8

Steps to Heaven

8

Steps to Heaven

A Simple Guide in Self-Awareness and Spiritual Development

A Journey for Everyone

Glyn Parry

Contact Publishing

-.-. —- -. - .- -.-. -

First published in the United Kingdom by:
Contact Publishing Ltd.
June 2004

British Library Cataloguing in Publication Data
A CIP catalogue record of this book is available from the British Library.

ISBN 0-9547020-0-X

Printed and Bound by
Samuelson & Nordhaus

Cover Design by Doverweb UK

Contact Publishing
Suite 346
176 Finchley Road
London NW3 6BT
www.contact-publishing.co.uk

Dedication

This book is dedicated to the higher self

Our guide

Contents

Step 3 Negative to positive: moving onwards and upwards from pain and loss

Step 4 Realisation: making your mind work for you

A.B.C.

Step 5 The preparation for your spiritual transition: the vision begins

1   Moving with the times
2   Learning to fight the vampires of spirituality
3   The essential reasons for protection
4   Trusting in your senses
5   Seeing your power
6   Mediation – Part I
7   The dreams and nightmares
8   Staying grounded

Step 6 The Unknown: exploring the mystical world

1   Psychics
2a Mediums/Spiritualists
 b The trans-medium
3   Clairvoyants/clairaudients
4   Tarot (the tarot cards)
5   The eighth chakra
6   Spiritual healing
7   Past lives
8   Deja vu

Step 7 Speaking to God: taking your journey a step further

Step 8 Your step

The truly blessed

A short poem

My dear friend you're heavenly beautiful
For your presence is the beauty
From one's heart
As like the sweet smells drifting
From the banks of God's most
Favourite and sacred rivers
You channel your thoughts
Through the light of the Lord
To which you are blessed
From the god of tranquility.
For time stands still
When you are around
So let the flavour of
Life pass through you
And all around
For to line the human mind
With compassion
Is to give the face purity.

Glyn Parry

Author's note

As you take yourself on this quest for higher spiritual knowledge, there are many key factors that have to be looked at and understood. Within this book your journey begins. This book offers you a step-by-step account of the main elements of awareness in a simple form. To be a spiritually aware human being you have to grow to appreciate so much more than you may already do. It is not possible to get there without dedication. I hope the simple passages can bring you that little bit closer to gaining the knowledge you need on your journey because, without first understanding the basic human life, you cannot understand your purpose or journey. Take only what you need from the text, as it is just a guide to help you along the way.

Somewhere in this book there will be a reflection, a reflection of you. It is up to you to recognise that it is you, and to be honest with yourself on your way to spiritual success: honest, honest, honest.

Good luck and God bless

Acknowledgements

I would like to say thank you to my mother for standing by me on my spiritual journey, the rest of my family and friends for believing in me, and of course my beautiful wife Ella for sharing the workload. Thanks to Anne at Contact Publishing for instigating what you will read; without her there would be no book to speak of. Last, but definitely not least, the world of spirit and all that have played a part in helping me to write this book.

Thank you and God bless.

Introduction Part 1

CONFUSED BY EVERYDAY LIFE, searching, wishing for a solution to just jump up and tap you on the back?

Everybody needs, everybody wants, everybody desires. There are just a few things that get in the way and that make us nervous, stressed generally, in pain. Some people call this ambition. Others say, "Be happy; content with what you have." The question is, how? How do we maintain a happy, healthy, content life without fear, and on top of that be consistent with it?

Well, this is what you will learn and hopefully will have achieved by the time you have finished this book.

We are constantly searching for happiness, whether it be through love, work, play or perhaps even within a world of negative actions. Let's face it, this book is not for everyone. It is for people of all ages who wish to be true to themselves.

As each day passes in all of our lives we miss so much, we have too much on our minds, too little time for our friends, our family or loved ones. It might sound mushy but here lies many of the answers to all of our questions of happiness within our selves.

I cannot tell you what you must do. I can only guide you as we walk this path together.

I can think of so many reasons why I could have chosen other paths in life. For example, it's easier to just fit into society. It's more enjoyable to go out clubbing, get drunk and roll into your house in the early hours of the morning, always putting yourself before others. But thankfully, I chose to listen very carefully to myself, my intuition, as people would call it.

Life can be emotionally draining at the best of times. It can pull us from left to right, up and down, and turn us inside out. This is how I felt my life was treating me before I looked for ways in which to change, to find my intuition.

As a child I went through many similar situations to a lot of other people: Heartbreak Hotel when my parents split up. Flunking school because of the desire to be angry with everyone. I then found myself on a pathway to self-destruction and sadness as I entered my early teens. There are many reasons why any one person wishes to find peace within. For me, it was my childhood. I chose to search out my true higher self to make sure I could learn how to forgive, to be strong, brave and most of all humble.

There are many different situations that are creating sadness in people right now. Whatever your situation, embrace it and fight for what you want. This is how I got to where I am now. But when I say fight, I don't mean with your fists or anger. I mean with love and wisdom.

I'm sometimes lost for words at how genuinely thankful I am to all the great people I have met on my journey, the people who gave me the internal power to find my higher self, my intuition. It's the pain that others have given me that opened the doorway to discovery. Without experiencing the hurt I felt in my early years could I have ever possibly achieved what I have right now. I'm not looking for sympathy. I would like you to understand that something great, something glorious nearly always comes from a tale of sadness.

For many years I have seen torn souls turn to pure grace. It is never easy but the bliss that awaits the one who finds true love and wisdom is magical.

My journey of self-discovery began when I was seventeen. That was when I decided to hang up my angry coat. It took me to different parts of the world and helped me to meet many wonderful people. I guess it was the need to search for peace of the heart that drew me to so many spiritual people. I found that the more I grew to understand the nature of spirituality the closer I came to my own awakening. I had great spiritual teachers who were, obvious to me now, destined to be part of my life. They embraced my fears and guided me through the pain I felt as a child. In doing so they gave me a whole new vibration. It enhanced my ability to stay positive, to separate the good from the bad.

I worked with different people for a couple of years before I felt I had achieved the goals set out in the book. I then found myself on the receiving end of other people's problems, and found that I was always able to help. When I was on my spiritual journey, finding my higher self and my intuition, didn't come easy. But I'm so glad I took the time to listen and understand the benefits of spiritual practices, for if I hadn't I wouldn't be writing this book. I hope that the wisdom that was passed on to me through the wonders of life can be passed on to you. I hope with all my heart that you enjoy unfolding your soul on this journey you are about to take. It only gets better.

Imagine, as you walk your path of life, you are a small bird flying from tree to tree, watching everyone and everything around you, knowing that if you take your eye off the moment for one second it could be all over. Imagine yourself as that small bird. You could be so free, able to glide through life with the greatest of ease without a care in the world. The bird is free because it has to be constantly aware. Its path in life is to feed its young and to care for its loved ones.

The bird is the part of us that sees all; the all-seeing, loving part of our personalities. My point is, without first achieving the understanding of the feeling of love, how can we truly connect with others? If we fear love, we will forever be questioning our purpose of life, because love is the true source of life, the reason for being here. As long as you remember that, you will see how the true intuition will always be readily available.

Note: Please do not skip any sections within the book if you desire positive results.

8

Steps to Heaven

The journey begins: addressing the fundamental issues of a greater existence

1 How positivity affects your life

WE ARE TOLD over and over again – by friends down the pub, people at church, and teachers at school – how we should run our lives. How do they know how we should run our lives?

We never seem to get told how to learn to be us, to grow inside ourselves. We are constantly being pushed down rather than being embraced. We are force-fed media garbage, scientific reasoning, philosophies and so on – you get the point.

This, sadly, is the state of the world as we know it. If a little bit more time was spent on each and every one of us throughout life, we would find it so much easier to see and feel what we really needed to, how to feel the love and support from others, how to understand the need for internal peace to gain external happiness. We would be able to see people around us striving to achieve their goals to create a brighter world.

Tip

Here's a little tip for you. Every Sunday, do a good deed. It doesn't really matter what – any type of good deed will do. Give something to charity. Help someone across the street. Say thank you. Just try it and see how you feel within yourself afterwards. You can give yourself a pat on the back for that.

I would like to stress a point that it's important for all of us to try to maintain happiness for others as well as ourselves. Be happy for other people. Whatever path they choose in life, be happy for them. The reason I felt I had to say that is that we could become a little bit caught up in ourselves. I do believe giving a positive thought to others strengthens our souls.

It is amazing how a word such as 'positive' is so often used by all of us: "Stay positive; be positive." The ironic thing is that most of us don't realise we are being negative rather than positive on a day-to-day basis.

Throughout my own life I've tried and tested the art of staying positive. It is important to know that every time you think a thought about someone, the energy passed from your subconscious to theirs is amazing. This is one of the ways in which I grew to understand how powerful positivity and negativity are.

I would sit down quietly and think about two different people. There was Jane, the one who I didn't really want to see, and Sam, the other one I did want to see. I would then send really positive thoughts to Jane and negative (not nasty, just negative) thoughts to Sam. I found that every time I did this it was always the same.

The person who I didn't wish to see (Jane), would call me or cross paths with me, where as the person I did wish to see (Sam), would not call or cross paths with me in any way.

When I would finally call my friend Sam, after two to three days or a week, I could tell by the tone of her voice that something was wrong. I would ask her if I'd done anything wrong or if she had any ill feeling towards me that she couldn't explain. It was always the same answer; she felt something was wrong but she couldn't put their finger on it. I would then explain what I had been doing – my little test – and she would always be amazed. How, just with pure concentration and focus, could I project enough positive or negative energy onto her to make her change the way she felt towards me? So I guess now you can see how important it is to try to focus on positive thoughts towards people in your everyday life. You'll find it helps a lot in making your life run smoother in all areas: love, work and play. Try it out. It may or may not work for you.

> ## Positive Focus Tip
>
> There are many ways to maintain a consistent positive focus. One of the simplest ways is to keep something on you at all times like a small present or a picture; something that you treasure or something that makes you feel good.

Some people might dismiss the exercise as pure rubbish. It's likely the people who say that, say it in a negative manner. There are many people who want to believe in something they do not understand but are too afraid. Positive thought process – turning your fears into triumphs by searching inside yourself – has always been available to us.

The greatest teachers are spread out over different areas of the world: Tibetans, Buddhists, and of course the North American Indians. These teachers are our spiritual guides.

The American Indians take being positive very seriously. They would chant and pray before they killed a wild animal so the spirit of the animal would be saved, not banished with fright and negativity. Doesn't it make you wonder, though, why a race of people, so positive and spiritual, would be slaughtered and nearly completely removed from the planet?

As wildly bizarre as it may sound, fear through ignorance is still occurring in different ways for every human being right now. As you read these words, more and more people are becoming afraid to be positive within their lives. It takes strength to be positive, to not talk behind someone's back with a group of friends, to not laugh at the underprivileged. If you do, just remember that is weakness, not strength in being positive.

Often people laugh or make fun of you if you are kind to other people. How bizarre is that? Just think to yourself how truly strange it is that the world can be in so much emotional ruin that people feel they have to act in such a way. If you want to be truly loved by others, don't stand with the weak to feel comfortable.

**Stand alone for as long need be,
until the people destined to stand with you arrive.**

2 Taking control of your life

TAKING CONTROL OF YOUR LIFE is something that needs to be planned, thought about and focused on. It is not something that will just happen.

A lot of people use the phrase, "I'll do it tomorrow." Hmm! How typical. The only problem is that quite often tomorrow never comes. This is where a lot of people go wrong. They find themselves on this emotional wheel going round and round and round, like a hamster in a cage. Everything needs to be done in stages. 'Rome wasn't built in a day!' There is definitely truth in that.

Imagine your life split up into eight different areas: love, your partner, friends, family, work, the past, the present and the future. Each area has to be looked at very carefully.

Firstly look at the area that seems to be dragging behind the others. This is the one you need to focus on first.

Let's say it's work; maybe, more specifically, your work colleagues make you feel as though you're not part of the team. You feel especially left out when they're having a laugh. Or the bottom line is you just don't fit in. Maybe it hasn't always been like that. Maybe it has.

Let's say it hasn't. Lets say it's just now, in this job. You're probably saying to yourself, "Why don't they like me? What have I done wrong?" The fact is you probably haven't done anything wrong at all. You're just changing. As we grow, our emotions change day to day, through experiences that are thrown at us. For example, relationships breaking apart, the death of a friend or loved one, or just the pressures of daily life.

Whatever is happening in your life, wherever you feel the problem is within the eight different areas, the answer is always waiting to be found within yourself.

The answer lies in your memory of the past. People say, "Don't live in the past, live in the present." That is only true for the people who have found and already worked out the answer for themselves. Live within the here and now, but look to the past for your answers.

If you feel your life isn't in order, taking the work area as the example, then it needs to be addressed. The answer lies in the past. The past is your greatest weapon. It's your own bible to yourself. It's where all the good times, all the bad times and all the day-to-day growing lives and breathes. If you made a mistake in the way you talked to someone at work yesterday, don't do the same today. If you didn't kiss your partner when you got home yesterday and they were moody all night, kiss them twice today. Learn from the past. Be your own man or woman. Don't ignore the problems of the past. Face them. It will be then – and only then – that you will start to see your life becoming much more easy to deal with in all of the eight areas.

**The past has the answers to your present,
and in turn will build the foundation to your future!**

3 Facing your demons

FACING OUR DEMONS is probably one of the most difficult things any one person has to do at some point in their life. It is such a valuable process, which grants so much more freedom to express emotion on many different levels.

It's so difficult because the demons are the fears, the place of no reason. Facing the demons only quickens the process to staying positive within you. So, as you can see, it's so incredibly important to at least try to find a way to work with them, negotiating with them.

Once again it's a day-to-day process of slowly unfolding your insecurities that need to be addressed, to be broken down. Do not try to understand

and conquer all your fears – meaning demons – at once. For some people, it will take years to finally free themselves from their demons.

The big question here is: Why? Why are we so afraid to look at parts of ourselves, which do nothing for us but cause us pain and suffering?

A lot of people seem to think that there is no need to address their fears. That is obviously so untrue, as nobody is perfect. Each moment we ignore our anger, envies, jealousy, etc., we build a mountain of problems that just take that much longer to climb.

The answer lies in moderation. A step-by-step procedure, which is not only beneficial to us, but also to others around us.

Emotions Exercise

It involves a pen and notepad, and preferably a secret place to hide what you write. All you need is about ten minutes a day. Jot down anything in the day that made you feel uncomfortable, angry, jealous, sad, alone... or anything that you feel you wish to write. Just write it. Check the clock and don't stop writing for ten minutes.

This step-by-step process allows your subconscious an escape route to the outer world. You will be shocked at what you write. Sometimes you will be upset by it, but this is very positive. This is the beginning of a much brighter existence for you. It will give you a sense of freedom.

This could be a lengthy process. Don't expect miracles overnight. The more you write about your emotions the closer you will get to really knowing yourself. You will see how releasing your negativity improves your well-being. The most satisfying thing is when you start to appreciate yourself. Starting to like yourself is a major breakthrough to facing your demons. In liking who you are, both good and bad, you will see how you are able to start liking and appreciating people around you. It's simple but it works, and it definitely helps.

4 Standing alone, but standing strong

THERE AREN'T THAT MANY PEOPLE who would admit to being content with spending a lot of time on their own. That's understandable, as some people would see that as kind of eccentric, like a hermit. In this section, you will achieve the knowledge that you do not have to be surrounded by people to be happy.

Standing alone basically means spending time on your own to contemplate your thoughts. Standing alone gives your conscious and subconscious mind a chance to breathe. For some, it may not be the easiest thing to do, but it will teach you a lot about yourself.

When you sit quietly do you find messages, answers or visions come to you? Maybe you don't notice them, yet they do come from your subconscious. We'll be talking a lot more about that later on.

It's worrying that the "fear" factors in our lives pull us in so many different directions that only harm us and teach us nothing. Standing alone is not wrong. Monks practice transcendental meditation for up to six months at a time. It's a form of meditation whereby they leave their conscious mind to meditate within their higher-self. It's all about growth. You don't have to have twenty good friends. Two or three are fine. If you have the energy and dedication to give to twenty friends and to give to work and play and love, equally, then I want to meet you.

Give yourself time for yourself. Let yourself recharge your batteries. Then, you will have much more energy to give to your three friends. Aim for quality rather than quantity. Stick by that and you'll never go wrong.

Standing alone gives you much more strength of character. You don't have to spend days and days on end alone, like a hermit. The odd day here and there will help you to start to understand yourself. Remember, what people can give to you is nothing compared to what you can give back when standing alone.

> ## Personal Time Exercise
>
> Plan to have one day to yourself, for yourself. Read, write, watch a few films, whatever you choose just be sure you are only with yourself.

5 Building the bridges to a free mind

THE BRIDGES ARE THE PATHWAYS between the conscious and subconscious mind. The subconscious mind is the place of true understanding. Many people believe that the subconscious part of our mind holds all the answers to the deepest questions, something you will in time have to discover for yourself. This book can only guide you on our journey together, not tell you what to do.

We are all destined to understand the paths we are given when the time is right. You may start to understand more about your inner soul, your intuition, by the end of the book. The only way to work the magic we have been given is to listen, truly listen, to our inner soul, our intuition. The bridges grant us this opportunity. How can you listen to your soul if you're partying 24/7 or working all hours? That is why it is so important to spend time by yourself.

Understand that not only do we have an ability to see, hear, touch, smell and taste, we also have on open 24-hour gateway to a world of truth. It has been said that time creates wisdom and understanding. That may be true for your everyday conscious mind, but there is so much more we can achieve and doors we can open, to further our own spiritual development in our daily lives.

As each day passes in your everyday life you'll always be given tests; tests to give you strength as you go on your journey. The bridges and the subconscious may sound daunting. It is very important for you to find a place in your conscious mind where you feel comfortable with yourself.

The more in tune you are with your feelings, yourself, the easier it will become to deal with the tests thrown at you each and every day. For example, finding out that your partner's cheating on you, or losing your mind through drugs. Either way

A wise man can only begin his journey, when his journey has begun!

6 The place of freedom (the magician)

OW MANY TIMES do you see people bicker, argue or upset others? Don't you ever ask yourself why? Why do they find it so necessary to fight amongst themselves? There is a simple explanation for this. They are not listening.

When you do listen, you will find the place of freedom. It separates you from the crowd, allowing you to understand not only yourself, but also others around you. We are all put here for a reason. Individually, we each have our own paths to take and our own mistakes to make. Sadly, the majority of people never find their true vocation in life. Knowing who you are enables you to see what you are and what your job or duty is on the earth. It might be that you are destined to be a window cleaner or a refuse collector. You may be destined to be a president or a movie star. Either way you will be what you will be.

It is a gift to be able to take every day as it comes, to release all wants and needs. To truly just be.

Magician Exercise

When you're trying to just be, and to listen to yourself, just stop; stop what you're doing and sit down, wherever you are, just relax. Imagine yourself as a magician. Focus on the place in your mind where nothing matters, where there are no worries or cares. Do it for as long as it takes until you feel the magic inside you. At this point you will probably start smiling. When you feel the sense of happiness flowing all over your body and mind, try to hold it. Hold it for as long as possible. Then, like a magician, imagine that you are throwing it into the world for others to feel.

A little magic will come back to you in many different ways. Each day you will start to feel more empowered within yourself by being the magician.

Once you have achieved this sense of freedom you will begin to understand things that didn't seem relative to you before. You will start to see people differently.

The people you know will become the people you knew.

7 Stepping out on your own

STEPPING OUT ON YOUR OWN is one of the most rewarding but difficult parts of your own self-development. It is very different to standing alone, in that this is the point where you keep your life the same. The difference is that you change the way your life works for you. Nothing in life ever comes easy, and if you're searching for a happier existence then you need to be strong and ready for the changes that will occur within you. Hopefully, many of you desire to better your emotional being and spiritual sanctuary. If you truly wish to be the ruler of you own destiny, your spiritual and emotional destiny that is, you must understand that creating a better, more stable emotional world for yourself does in turn separate you from the world you once knew and, in turn, the way you see others. Do you wish to take the challenge? If so, step out to find your true path and read on.

8 Creating the strength

A MAN ONCE ADVISED ME to not let slip when I am sad or vulnerable. He said that, when others have not yet started their journey of self-discovery, they are still battling with their fears and often their fears and insecurities can stop them being honest in their actions. He said if that were the case, they may take advantage of my vulnerability. He said that witnessing the pain in me could possibly be a reflection in themselves. Therefore, they will often do anything else before letting me see them in a more naked form of emotion, because then they do not have to admit there is a problem. That type of fear could come out all twisted, and may be derogatory in the way they express themselves to me, due to the fear. The only positive benefit that comes from that kind of fear is that we have the ability to reverse the fear and instead, create strength. "Sticks and stones may break my bones." You will have heard that saying before. It sums up why the world needs more spiritually able people walking it than ever before.

So far we have talked about positivity, taking control of your life, standing alone, facing your demons, building your bridges to a free mind, the place of freedom and stepping out on your own. These are all parts of the circle of strength, the strength that will surround you if you take note and remember to be aware of the changes in yourself and your life around you.

The foundation: overcoming your soul fears

2

1 Acorns to oak trees

FOR SOME PEOPLE the thought of love can be a truly terrifying thing. We love to run from love. It's the fear of someone else taking advantage of our vulnerability. At the time in our lives when we are tender and young we have no reason to fear. We are warm and confident in our domain; free from the stresses and experiences we get to claim through our lives as adults.

We know why we run from love, we know how to keep love at arm's length. But do we know the benefits of love? Everybody at some stage in their adult life will experience some form of love, whether from a parent, a friend, a partner or even an animal. The reason for talking about love right here at the beginning of your journey is this: you have bought this book to hope to find the solutions to your state of mind and answers to how you feel about yourself and your life. You are hoping to read something magical in the text that will transform your life into some supreme vision of peace and tranquility. Remember, this book can only guide you.

So, let's go back to the beginning. To the most important issue of all: love. Love is where the spiritual development starts. Love is the foundation. This is the acorn stage. Let love guide you to follow through with your wish to achieve peace within and become an oak tree – the largest, most elegant oak tree in your life.

Finding solutions to problems is always challenging. Simply knowing whether you are making the right decisions is hard enough. Know when to stop and listen, have faith in your choice, and follow through, no matter what…well, that's another story. What you need to ask yourself is, how badly do you want this new life you're wishing for? How much are you willing to give up? How many changes are you realistically going to make to better your existence? Once you have made your decision, then read on. If you have decided to follow through and leave nothing to chance, then you are without doubt walking the road to happiness.

On the earth plane we have a fairly short lifespan, compared to other creatures such as the giant tortoise that can live for 200 years, so our chances of success, spiritual success, are that much slimmer, purely because of our day-to-day living. The first and hardest task in spiritual awareness is making the commitment. If you have chosen to dedicate time in your life to spiritual development then you are well on your way, because the first and hardest task in spiritual awareness is making the commitment.

Earlier, you read briefly about elements of strength and ways in which we can all become more positive in our outlook. Do not overlook that section, as being positive is the key. Without it, there is no spiritual development.

Positivity Exercise

Cast your mind back to a moment when you felt very positive. It can be the smallest of images. Focus on the thought. Try to hold the thought until it becomes a feeling. If you are feeling it, you have connected an element of love to the memory or vision.

The reason for this exercise was purely to let you see that if you are able to maintain a positive thought and feeling at the same time, then you are able to experience love. Love and positivity run in the same pool of emotions.

Now focus on the reasons you wish to change your outlook, and what has been stopping you. Hopefully you've understood the importance of love and positivity combined with thought, and you are ready to face with open arms the truths about yourself.

Honesty Exercise

This is where you look at yourself and say "Why is it that I wish to change?" Is it that you're just fed up with life, or is it that you're fed up with you? Maybe you just want to create a point of clarity in your life. Be honest with yourself.

Honesty is the only way to clear away the old to make way for the new. If you find it difficult, don't worry. Right here and now, only you and I exist so it's okay. Being honest with yourself also ties in to what has been stopping you from moving forward spiritually. The answer is you. Nobody else. Some of you will probably say, "No, it's not. It's not me. It's my wife." Or, "It's my family. They don't give me enough space." Or, "My job's too demanding. I don't have time because the kids are always begging for my attention." I would say it's best to not blame anyone else but yourself for not getting to a point in life that you wish to.

A new beginning will only transpire if someone is present to live in it.

Once you've practised being honest with yourself, ask yourself if any of the situations or fears that you think were holding you back need love and positivity to develop. It's back to the same question again, "Is it me, or is it them? I'm sure I was giving enough and not taking." If you want a more peaceful and spiritual life, then you need to create that around yourself by projecting that emotion onto everyone around you. Give love; receive love. Receive love; give love. As long as that flow of energy is being passed between you and anyone around, you are left with so much more space to develop your spiritual side. Everyone will be happy. Sometimes it can seem as though you're on a treadmill just going round and round. It is always more difficult to get started when life is like that.

Relaxation Suggestion

Just give yourself more time. A great way of relaxing your mind after a stressful day is to sit somewhere quiet and burn a couple of red candles and lavender if you have them. Let your mind wander and think of nothing. It's not easy at first, but practice makes perfect.

I always find candles help to create an atmosphere of relaxation. They also give a sense of spiritual peace. A relaxed atmosphere sets me up for a day of positivity.

Another point needs to be addressed before we move on. When making your decision for a better spiritual life, make sure you are making it for the right reasons. Some people have been known to brag about how being more spiritually aware has given them greater financial gain. This is untrue. Creating a brighter, more spiritual outlook in your life is purely about bettering the way you feel and how you see the world.

To walk the path of spiritual development for financial gain is to burn the bridge that still remains.

Let's move on.

2 Having faith

FAITH. WHAT A WORD. It gets thrown around by so many different types of people that it seems to have been lost somewhere.

Right now in the world many religions are dictating, using the word faith. Much harm has been thrust upon people by using fear in faith. Why is it that so many hundreds of thousands of people have started doubting faith in their religions on a global scale? Why is it that the average teenager on the street would rather fight amongst his or her friends, without a thought for others, rather than have faith in themselves?

The word faith sounds ugly to a lot of people because of religion. Well, self-belief doesn't, and that's what we are here to achieve. Spiritual development is based on faith and self-belief. It's about time we changed the way we see faith and start seeing it for its purity, here and now.

Having faith does not have to be an archaic affair. We don't have to wear robes and sing hymns to have faith. If you wish to do that, however, that is your choice. My point here is that faith needs to be shared. Shared with the people. Everyone needs faith: faith in themselves and faith in life. As we move on through the book, you will see how faith becomes an incredibly significant part of spiritual clarity.

I would like to point out that I do not wish to slander any religions or beliefs, as I believe in unconditional love. However, I do believe it's time we opened our eyes to the desperate need for a global faith before the world turns on its head.

The point of this book is to help people to understand what is right and what is wrong, to have self-belief and to understand the sense of responsibility they have to others. That is what spiritual development is all about. Learning to have faith in a faithless world.

We are all under the same sky and yet we have our own choices to make. We all have a choice to learn to understand faith and, with that, the healing powers that come with self-belief. The aim is to give you a real chance to test just how much self-belief you have. It's all about you. There's no one here to tell you what, how or when you must do something. There is no one to push you in any direction that you don't wish to go in. This book should help you see things you already know in a different light. Some things you may know, some you may not.

Remember, you are your own leader. Nothing can stop you fulfilling your goals. You have the ability to love and be loved. No one can thrust any kind of faith onto you as you already have your own.

As we have already discussed, knowledge and wisdom comes from an internal source, as does faith, so it is important to remember that people will try to persuade you to change. In life, that is the nature of the faithless. They are here to bring you down.

The weak are the faithless people who create negativity, but we must always remember to forgive. Forgiving makes us stronger.

Faith has been frowned upon for many years now by our younger generations. It is very important to help the children of the future to see faith, not as some religious mumbo-jumbo, but as something much more relative to their lifestyles and cultures. I feel there's a great need for an input of faith within society as a whole, but the children of tomorrow should be the main focus. So if you are under sixteen and you are reading this book, understand that you no longer have to go to Sunday school or attend a church to understand faith. Attending church can be a beautiful experience, but if you feel that your belief, your faith in yourself, is disappearing, then it's up to you to decide where your journey lies. The faith of tomorrow is not within four walls but on the streets, in the eyes of the people, and all around us. The faith of tomorrow can only be born if the children of today learn to walk with the faith of today.

It's time to spread the word that faith is freedom and faith is love, and faith is being you.

Without first having faith in yourself, can you truly have faith in others? Without faith, there is no future. It's brutal, but it's the reality of today. We are seeing more and more murders, rapes and criminal activities in our world than ever before. A large proportion of this crime is coming from our younger generation. Again, whoever reads this book must try to at least pass the idea of faith for today to others as a good thing. That way, the future of our children will be so much brighter, just by having a little bit of faith.

3 Forgiveness

LIFE CAN BE a very complicated place, full of situations that create a handful of sad times. Sometimes the situations created are not created by us. Sometimes they are completely out of our control. Nobody can ever say they are perfect. In a non-perfect world with non-perfect people, non-perfect events transpire. One of the significant reasons for spiritual development is awareness. All that we have talked about so far gives simple guidelines to many different factors, which when all put together, play a part in awareness. The more aware we are, the easier it is to see things on a much clearer level. We cannot only see things clearer but we can also make them more positive.

The world is fueled by hatred in many ways, like war, crime and religion. Because of this, there are millions of people walking the earth feeling bitter, let down, rejected and betrayed. This is why it is so important that a new spiritual revolution is given the chance to manifest itself, through us.

There are hundreds of thousands of people fighting for a more spiritual and positive world and I'm hoping that you are one of them. Before you can be that spiritual leader of awareness in your own right, you have to be able to forgive. It can be incredibly difficult to forgive someone at this early stage of your journey. That is why it is written within the foundation so early in the book.

What you need to ask yourself is, are you somebody who finds it hard to forgive? Why do you find it hard? If your answer is an overwhelming sense of anger or sadness then that's what you must overcome.

Forgiveness is like a wall.
Once you break it down, you are able to see.

Forgiveness is not the answer to your problem, though. To forgive is just the beginning of the new path that will be walked upon from the moment you do forgive. You must not look upon forgiveness as the weakness in you. It is the strength. The person or people you need to forgive are in many cases not wrong for what they have done, but merely because they took a wrong turning on their path of life. It is up to us to help guide them back on the right track. You see, forgiveness may be the beginning of a new journey but it is just a simple stepping-stone to a brighter future. I forgave a friend who betrayed me. We are now better friends than ever. Forgive to move on.

It can be very difficult to forgive someone who has wronged you. Just remember that sometimes, just sometimes, you may be the one to do wrong to them. So, you see, it works both ways. We as a human race must all learn to forgive before the world's emotional economy becomes completely bankrupt.

It's important for you to know that I know how difficult it can be to forgive somebody who has really hurt you. Feuds between friends or family members can go on for years. But the brutal truth is, as mentioned in, 'Acorns to oak trees,' that everybody needs love. It is important to put your anger aside and look at the situation between yourself and the person or people in question. Really look at them. Look at them like you don't know them. See their pain, their dissolution in life. It's up to you to rise above and seek the higher plane of spiritual awareness, because in this life we get one chance. Take that chance and start trying to give in to forgiveness and let people back into your life. As good a place as any to start forgiving is in the home. If you don't live with your family, then start with a friend or maybe a work colleague you feel has let you down. It's quite important, like anything in life, to start small. Don't run before you can walk. As all the different areas of your journey start to make sense, the book won't be divided into separate passages of information. It will become one large pool of knowledge for you to dip into at any time. But for now, let's start small.

Forgiveness Exercise

You probably know who you need to forgive. Right then, let's take the first step. It's hard, but think of the rewards of a more peaceful life. Imagine the person's face in your mind. Think back to a time before you had your feud, when things were still good and fun was being had. Simply focus on that image for a couple of minutes until you're certain that your feelings for that person feel good. At the exact moment of feeling good, imagine a line of silk or something of your choosing going from your mind to theirs. Now, imagine a small envelope with a piece of paper inside it. On the piece of paper it simply says, "Dear friend will you please forgive me." Now imagine the letter gliding along the silk line all the way to the mind of the other person.

You see, to forgive in just everyday thought can be pretty much impossible. Nothing will have changed about the way in which you see this person. But if you create a new visual space, place and situation in your mind that allows forgiveness to take place you can start the process of forgiveness. It may sound rather strange, but you can only but try. If it doesn't seem to help you, then maybe it's just helping the other person. There it is: your beginning of forgiveness.

4 The leopard and the spots

WE SEE CHANGE ALL AROUND US every day. We are expected to change to suit our environment. So why is it that we fear change so much?

It's true that for most of us we want to change some, if not a lot of ourselves because we are unhappy. Change is evolution; change is inevitable. So why do we find it so hard to go with the flow when change occurs?

Change is once again a fear, a fear that we are going to lose the control we have built up over certain areas of our lives. It is often very difficult for some people to see change as a good thing, yet we are all trying to change in some way or another. We accept that the day turns to night and that summer turns to winter. So, why is it that when change occurs in our personal lives, change that is out of our hands, we panic? Is it because we don't know what's coming with the change, or is it that we don't have trust in what the future holds? Either way we need to start accepting that change will occur and that it can often be a very good thing. Ask yourself why you are reading this book. To stay exactly the same?

We want to change our lives when we want to change our lives. That's totally fair. We want to take from life only the good bits. We want to not be told of change coming, but just to create change.

You see, we as humans want to dominate by nature. It's in our DNA to dominate. But as we are all here to try to better our lives, we need to accept change. Go with it. The only way to truly learn to live with change is to embrace it. If we wish to evolve spiritually then we must embrace the changes that occur within us. If we try to control and dominate change, we will be left with only a fraction of the truth of the change that occurred.

As you read, changes will be happening within your conscious and subconscious constantly. If you choose to make positive decisions in your life based on what you have read, then change will occur for the better in you. You see, people say a leopard can't change its spots. Maybe it can't change its spots, but it can certainly blend into its surroundings. That's what you must do: change and blend. The more hidden you are within the human race, the more time and opportunity you have to create a more positive world for yourself. So, the story of a leopard not changing its spots may be true in a literal sense, but as for honing one's ability to better their outlook, then no, everyone can change.

As the changes occur, which they will, it is important that you learn to trust in the change. As you grow with learning so your emotional and mental senses will grow. You will become acutely more vulnerable because your senses will be that much more open. Once again, it's important to trust. Trust in what is taking place within you. Believe in yourself and in the changes that are taking place. Some changes may seem more painful than others because that is the nature of growth. No pain no gain. But you must go with this change.

Just as in, 'Standing alone, but standing strong,' change will create a kind of separation between you and others around you. You will want to shout out loud to everyone as you progress about your fantastic new developments.

> ## Tip
>
> It's much safer for you if you keep yourself to yourself about the new ways in which you are see things and the new feelings that you are experiencing. Blend in to your environment. Do not bring attention to yourself on your journey.

There are many jealous people out there in the world waiting to pull you down or prove you wrong. Learning to trust change can be a lengthy process as it takes every ounce of belief in yourself to allow change to happen. Being able to release any doubts or fears that you have is difficult for anyone. Just believing one hundred percent that what ever will be will be takes a lot out of anyone.

To create that kind of power in your mind is tough, but possible. It takes a great deal of mental thought.

> ## Mental Power Exercise
>
> Think of nothing; throw all of your fears and worries into that dark, forgettable space. At first, the fears may come flying back into your mind. But, practice will make perfect. The more you push away the fears and worries that you hold for the future, the stronger you will become. About five minutes a day, if possible, is recommended to create that pattern of thought in your mind. Throw away the fear to create change.

Once you have mastered the thought process just discussed, it will become a lot more plausible for things to just happen in your life, leaving you a lot more fulfilled. So much of what transpires with changes in your life come completely from the process of thought, from the moment you wake to what you want to dream about when you are about to sleep. Our lives are dominated by change, so control your ego with thought and let change guide you to a better world.

5 Karma

IF **YOU ARE** someone who is trying to overcome a lifetime of failure, then you are at the right stage in the book.

In this passage we will talk about karma, and the effects it has on everyone at some time in their life.

We know that karma is supposed to be something to fear. We know that if you do wrong to someone, you will get bad karma. But do we know why, and how we can turn it around?

Karma is a word of great meaning that has been talked about and feared by many spiritual leaders for hundreds of years. For many cultures, karma is an energy most feared. Karma lives up in the heavens with the gods and is sent down to punish people for their wrongdoing. American Indians say that they have seen the spirit of karma riding the wind and pray that karma is blown away by positive thought. They believe karma is the spirit of Man sent from another life to punish us. If we are unable to see the path that awaits us, we are not ready to walk it. If we do wrong to others and do not try to change, we cannot be forgiven by karma. Therefore, we are not ready, and the spirit of karma will come to stop us in our tracks until the time when we have learnt the great rules of life. Some people are very unlucky, and if they never learn the great rules of life, love, faith, forgiveness, etc., the spirit of karma will continue to follow them from one life to the next. You may have to live many lives before the spirit of karma sets you free.

There is a purpose for everyone in life and yours may be karma. You may have been shown all the signs, but not recognised them. The signs are simple. For example, your career is not moving forwards, you find yourself feeling lonely no matter how many friends you have, or there is much illness in you or your family. The American Indians are great believers in giving to the karma spirit. They chant for hours to give the karma spirit free reign to choose its host. You see, you can't fight karma but you can send it on its way. It is up to you. If you do find yourself feeling bitter towards someone, address why and try to correct it. Don't become selfish in your ways. Try to put people's feelings first. Don't lie and cheat for self gain. Basically, be good to others and all creatures walking the earth, or the karma spirit may have to visit you.

You will achieve a much deeper understanding by the time you are truly on your spiritual journey, an understanding that will never question the goodness that you feel able to give. Of course, we all have our 'off days' when we are snappy and grumpy. This is the big test, the test of 'separating the men from the boys.' Don't let karma get to you: get to it first. With positivity and love, show the spirit you appreciate its worth.

The Indians say that the karma spirit could also have been following you through many lives and that it is important to send positive thought out as light in the mind.

> ## Karma Exercise
>
> Send white light out through your mind to create a kind of safety net for anything. Sending it to the karma spirit means that wherever it lands, it will give the host a softer landing.

You cannot stop karma at work. It's a pure entity that is part of evolution. Just remember you can help yourself. Always remember that.

As we all know how difficult it is to be good at all times it's probably beneficial to take heed in what the Indians say. At any time after an action of badness occurs, sit quietly and imagine the karma spirit. Then imagine a beam of white light surrounding the spirit while sending out as much positive energy as possible. Do this for as long as you wish.

Don't give in to it and say, "Oh forget this. I'll be fine," because karma is very real, very real indeed. We only live once on this earth, so let's make this one life a good one for us and for others.

6 Giving to get

THROUGHOUT TIME, we have evolved to create a much greater world for ourselves. We live to love and love to give. We throw ourselves into the most compromising of situations, just to move forward. We duck and dive and scheme to fulfill our most material of desires, never actually satisfying the true nature of our goal. We push and push in any way we can to achieve the house, the car, the second house, the designer clothes, the new promotion, and so on. How many of us give to others with only a thought of true unconditional giving in our hearts and minds? How many of us can't admit that we nearly always give something from the smallest gift to a house for the kids with the thought of always being able to get something back? You may say, "Well, I did give the house or car to my son or daughter unconditionally." Then a heated argument erupts and you shout out, "What about the car? What about the house? I did that for you, now you can do this for me."

It's like a minefield. Giving to anyone and expecting to get back will only ever cause major explosions amongst colleagues, friends or family. Nine times out of ten someone will eventually feel rejected or let down because they were expecting something in return.

Giving is about showing someone that you care. It's your opportunity to show that person, no matter who they are, that you are a friend to them and that their friendship means something.

The truth is, this subject once again boils down to inner peace. If you give only to feel that you deserve a return, surely that means that you are not content with yourself or your life? If you feel that you have to get something back, then what portion of yourself is not fulfilled?

Let's talk a bit about rejection. Rejection is experienced so much in our lives because we have so little faith in ourselves. Why should anyone feel rejected when in fact there is nothing to reject? We can stand on our own two feet, breathe, laugh, smile, love and live. So why would we feel that someone could reject that? Rejection is purely an issue that manages to manifest itself in our minds when we feel weak and vulnerable. Now, if we are happy and content with ourselves we wouldn't feel rejected, right? So, life should be how we wish it to be. Therefore we wouldn't have to feel rejected when we didn't get anything back. If that is the case, there is no room for rejection – particularly if we give unconditionally. To truly be unconditional in your actions means you have total control of rejection. It simply does not exist.

So it's easy to see how giving can create an awful lot of problems if done in an incorrect way. Honour yourself by staying true to the person or people you are giving to. Don't expect anything in return. They will honour you for it.

It really is about taking one breath at a time, one step at a time. Just knowing that you always feel the need to give in the hope of getting something back means that you are half way there. You've already recognised that there is an issue. This is a great achievement. Most of the giving-to-get issues are created at work. "I'll do that for you if you do this for me." Anyone walking this planet would feel a great deal better if they achieved something off their own back, rather than knowing their position in life came from giving an extensive amount just to move forwards.

It's not easy in the world. A part of our life is politically run. Try to achieve a sense of individuality. Know that you can stand on your own two feet without giving-to-get will make you feel so much better in yourself. Then maybe we can have some leaders in the world, rather than so many followers, because we all know how everyone races for the same treasures. This may sound as though we're going off the beaten track, but it's all relative to giving. Become a true giver and discover yourself, not a taker who never became themself.

You may be saying to yourself right now, "Why do I have to think about this issue? Why is it so important for me? It can't really affect my life – surely not?" Well, that is up to you to decide. But there is a fairly simple way of giving yourself a chance to try.

> **Giving Exercise**
>
> Try to give something – anything – to anyone. Just for the pure sake of it. For no other reason than to just give. Try something really easy at first, like buying a card or candles from a charity shop. That way you get something because you've paid for it, but you still give because your money goes to help orphans.

A lot of people reading this part of the book are probably thinking, "That's not me; I always give unconditionally." All I'm saying is just be sure you are, because it's not me who will be feeling rejected when I don't get back from something I gave.

7 Betrayal

BEING BETRAYED is one of the toughest challenges anyone has to go through in life. It might appear that there is no possible solution to stop betrayal. Have you looked carefully though?

We walk forward in life rarely thinking about the consequences. We often find ourselves walking into situation after situation with friends and partners, not seeing the signs that are clearly being shown to us.

I was in a shop one day a few years ago. A beautiful lady said to me, "We can only become the betrayed if we let betrayal get the better of us." And I said, "Yes, okay, I see that." Then she said, "People can't often see that they are being betrayed, because they are blinded by physical or mental illusion," as she gave me my change. By this point I didn't really know where she was going with this. Why would she be talking about this subject? She then told me she was working part-time and that she was studying forms of human behaviour. She then said to me, "Do you think you would be able to be betrayed without even noticing, right under your nose?" "No, no of course not," I said. It was at that point she asked me to take the money out of my pocket, and count the change that she had given me. I was ten pounds short. She told me that she felt that I was an open person and that it would be okay to test me in this way. It was something so simple, but so true. I was totally betrayed by her. She could have lied and told me that she did give me the right change. I could have done nothing about it, apart from being ten pounds out of pocket.

This may all sound a bit basic, but for many people this is exactly how we become betrayed by others – by the way someone looks, as I was in the shop, or by what somebody tells us. One of the key forms of betrayal is promises; promises that are made to break.

It's all about the way in which we see things: seeing them for what they are, or for what we believe them to be. It's so, so important to be cautious about the changes we make in our lives. Be aware of your decisions at all times. Only ever make decisions when you are on an even keel; neither angry, nor sad, nor happy. Make decisions that alter the path of your life when you're relaxed and feeling balanced.

On a deeper level, we have betrayal of love. Now, this is so much more painful. When a partner or very close friend decides that they are going to stab you in the back by having an affair, or, as a friend hurting you in such a way that you can't go back. There are so many factors to betrayal and it is often very difficult to see the factors.

It is very often the case that we do set ourselves up for betrayal. We need to look for the points, which make us feel uncomfortable in others.

Look for signs of denial in people, in their actions towards you. Always look past the exterior. Try to see inside the person in question. Sometimes it's incredibly hard to see the real person in front of you because they have learnt to camouflage the signs of betrayal. There are always going to be times in life where we miss something and somebody betrays us. We can only try to look that little bit closer to avoid betrayal.

If you are the type of person who decides that, no matter what, you are going to jump into a situation feet first, then it's best to always have boundaries for yourself: the amount that you are prepared to take or the amount that you can give to another person. For example, if you allow your partner to nag you when you want to go out for a drink with friends, eventually you will end up in an argument. This is because you did not create a boundary. To do so, you simply say no. If you find yourself having to explain for hours on end about what time you will be home and who you will be with, you will be on a downward slope. For a lot of people, this is where you will be. This is only because it's very difficult to have to think of setting out boundaries at the beginning of your relationship, when love is overwhelming. At the end of the day it is up to you. Set your boundaries at the beginning of the relationship – or wait until it gets so bad that you have to say no. Try to get used to setting boundaries in your mind at the beginning of a new relationship. It will save you pain that you don't need to experience. Remember, people don't like change. Betrayal can only happen if you let it. Therefore make sure you are able to stand strong in decisions you make about the way in which you see the relationship running smoothly. Obviously, communication helps when finding good positive ground within a relationship of any kind.

It is very important that you are aware of your boundaries when you form a friendship or a romantic relationship. Know when to say no, as not being able to say no is very often one of the major causes of betrayal. What we are talking about doesn't really affect a couple with a harmonious relationship, but you never know. It might come in handy.

As we've talked about before, we often set ourselves up for a fall. We set ourselves up for betrayal. If you find that you have got to that point in a relationship and you can't say no, then you must read on. Betrayal is what happens when you don't set boundaries within your mind in a relationship.

It can't be stressed how important it is to know what you are able to give and take.

If you find yourself always giving in a relationship, it is human nature for the other person in the relationship to take you for granted. It makes you feel terrible about yourself, and makes you worry that the future doesn't look so bright. This is very common in many relationships, so do not feel that you are the odd one out. You might be one of the lucky ones who have managed to work out your boundaries further into your relationship. This is great. If you haven't set your boundaries, the pain can become much too great to deal with on a day-to-day basis, especially if there is a lack of communication.

Learning to say no is just one element of a long-lasting relationship. So, if you are entering into a new partnership or friendship, be ready to say no if you truly don't want to do something they ask. When you haven't learnt to lay boundaries, you end up creating the betrayal yourself. The less we stand our ground and give only what we feel we can, the more chance we give our partner or friend to take advantage of our heart. There will come a point that we decide to make a stand, but at that point, it is often too late. They won't understand why you are then saying no because they are so used to getting what they want. They can often feel betrayed and angry themselves. It is at that point that your partner or friend will seek other places to lay their hat. It can be very difficult to fine-tune the way in which you deal with issues that could cause betrayal on a day-to-day basis. Just remember, you must not blame your friend or partner for leaving your life peacefully or abruptly if you never give them a choice or chance.

> **Tip**
>
> Look for signs that you might end up being betrayed. If you see or feel them make a choice whether you wish to enter the relationship or not. If you choose to enter the relationship, have your boundaries worked out in your mind. Be aware that your actions can create a chain reaction to betrayal. Try to be honest in yourself and do not promise anything you can't stick to. If you feel you do not have to worry, that betrayal does not stand by your side, stay aware, because betrayal has no sides.

Betrayal is what it is, and it's in all of us.

8 The green-eyed monster

THE GREEN-EYED MONSTER is jealousy. Jealousy kills any type of relationship. Jealousy will rip through any friendship or partnership like a bush fire rips through trees.

The most amazing thing about jealousy is that it's not only a manifestation of bitterness and anger but it is also so finely tuned by so many people on this earth. Jealousy is like a disease. It will eat into your confidence, into your heart and soul and into your mind, consciously and subconsciously. So many of the passages talked about in this book relate closely to each other, as there are many different parts of one whole person – you. That's why jealously has to be talked about. Why be jealous of someone else? Why not just be truly happy for them?

What really makes us so weak in our personalities that we feel the need to have to worry that someone is bettering us in life? Where has our self-belief gone?

Like any type of fear, jealousy has to be dealt with. Everybody talks about how we can't change, how if we are a jealous person then we will always be a jealous person. I feel very fortunate that jealousy is something that I've never had to address in my personality. But, I have known many others that have. For example, I remember a time about thirteen years ago, when I was away in a different country doing various spiritual practices. I had been there about a week, and had helped about thirty different people with spiritual advice.

I remember sitting with this lady called Sue, answering a lot of her questions. She seemed over the moon at the advice I had given her. I remember that Sue was the last person I saw that day. I can see it so clearly, for what happened next shocked and hurt me.

There was a phone call. It was a man threatening me with violence if I did not leave. He told me that I was not the man that I made out I was. He told me that he was the boyfriend of Sue. I felt it was not worth staying there, and decided to leave. Just before I left there was another call. It was Sue. She couldn't apologise enough. She explained that her boyfriend was desperately trying to become a spiritual reader. She explained that he was extremely jealous. She said that she had never seen him so angry as he was when she was telling him the great things I had told her.

As you can imagine, I was fairly upset by this. But, people will be people.

If you are a very jealous person, or maybe just somebody who gets jealous occasionally, then it would be wise for you to read this section. Remember, it's only you and I here together, so you can be honest with yourself. The funny thing is that nearly every person I've ever met who is a jealous type of person will never admit it. "Are you a jealous person?"

"Who? Me? No, I'm never jealous." They deny it because they know jealousy equals weakness. If you show your jealousy to others then you have shown them how little you believe in who you are, what you are and what you are able to achieve. A wise thing to remember is that nobody's perfect. You will have things that others don't and other people will have things that you don't. It's that simple.

What surprises me is how many ways in which jealousy can take hold. You wouldn't think that people would be jealous because their friend has a bigger house or a better car. Unfortunately, sometimes that is the case. Sometimes, though, jealousy is of the person! It could be in the way they look or the way they run their lives or what they achieve emotionally, girlfriends and boyfriends, etc. What is amazing is that the jealous person doesn't see that all the time they spend being jealous is time wasted. If they put that energy into themselves positively, they too may be in identical circumstances as the person for whom they feel jealousy.

The first key is: stay focused.

Banishing Jealousy Exercise: part 1

Concentrate on one thing that you feel is great or that you are happy with in your life. You need to try to maintain an inner focus rather than letting your mind wander, thinking about the great things that are happening in the lives of others. Once you have thought of just one thing that's pleasing to you in your life, think about why you're so happy about this thing. Remember exactly when you realised it, and why it makes you feel content. It could be your car, your hair, a pair of shoes, or love. What ever it is, be thankful for it. Think to yourself how grateful you are to have this thing.

The second key to ridding yourself of jealousy is appreciation.

Banishing Jealousy Exercise: part 2

Now appreciate that you have this thing in your life. Recognise how lucky you are, not how unlucky you are because you know someone with a bigger, better or more beautiful thing. Just simply, how lucky you are. No matter how unlucky you feel, I can pretty much guarantee you that there is someone else in life that is worse off than you.

A lot of jealous people will say, "It's not fair. How come they can have that and I can't?" When you think about it, it's really quite pathetic, isn't it? It's so easy to forget just how lucky we are. This may seem fairly harsh, but there is no point in running from the actual truth of the matter.

Being jealous is not something that you can take hold of and conquer straight away. If you are a jealous person it is important for you to realise and remember that being jealous will only end up hurting you in the end. Jealousy is like a roundabout. Once you're on it, it's hard to get off.

A good way to see how lucky you are in life is to start trying to look for people on the street who are worse off than you and not the ones who seem better off. If that doesn't work, go to a library and look up books on disease, malnutrition and the homeless. Don't be afraid to be thankful, being thankful has no weakness.

Life is short on the earth for all of us, so don't let the good fortune of others ruin your time here.

Enjoy their happiness and, most of all, enjoy yours.

Negative to positive: moving onwards and upwards from pain and loss

1 The beginning

FOR MANY YEARS people have fought for what they own. We only get one chance in this life to truly make the most of our happiness with others. From the day we are born we are searching, learning, and building a foundation to make our future so much brighter than that of everyone else.

It is important that we try to understand how to give what needs to be given emotionally as well as materially to others and to ourselves. We all need, as a human race, to reach much higher goals with values for ourselves and for others. People talk about time slipping away. They talk of the end of the world. Imagine if there isn't going to be an end? What if it's more like a transition? Each individual human being has their lessons set and their tests to pass. The truly bizarre thing is each and every one of us will actually never know. We only know the time between birth and death. Maybe we are completely missing the big picture as to what all of our lives together really mean to this planet. You can only do what you can, and that is a given.

How many times do you wish your life was way different from what it is? "I wish we could live in another country," "I wish we could have more money," "I wish I was better looking or didn't have to work." You must always remember you can have exactly what you want, but, what you want may not necessarily be what you need. Needs are often merely desires. Desires are often just needs to fill voids in one's life.

2 Reversing your wants and needs

REVERSING YOUR WANTS AND NEEDS is about telling yourself that whatever it is you really want, you don't really want. "Hey! Hang on," you are probably saying, "what is he talking about?" Well, every time you want something – really want something – you have to imagine in your mind that you don't care about it, imagine that you have all you need. It may be a new job, a new car, a holiday or even a new partner. The energy going outwards from you when wanting and needing so much actually has the reverse affect. It turns into energy of desperation, and desperation breeds loss.

For example, if you are going for an interview for a new job, do not be desperate. If you act in a desperate manner when being interviewed, it will show. This will automatically create a sense of lack of belief in yourself. The interviewer will recognise the signs that you're giving off. He will then, more than likely, cross you off his list of future employees. Therefore you are creating a loss for yourself. You may be the best person for the job. If you are, know it. Do not let desperation show itself to others. It is probably the most difficult process I have had to encounter in my own life because it takes so much will-power and determination to achieve the opposite. For example, the most difficult achievement I had to conquer was giving up smoking. Smoking creates ultimate desperation. The more you smoke, the more you need to smoke. If you don't get the next fix you can become very, very desperate, therefore creating no end to loss. Smoking is a perfect example of how strong you need to be, how much will-power you need to have to give up and create the opposite of desperate. This is all about the mind. When you get to the point when you can walk away from your wants and needs, you will get what you want and need. It seems like a bit of a brain-stormer, but over time you will see the rewards of reversing the desperation.

3 The consistency

UNDERSTANDING WHAT HAS JUST BEEN SAID and putting it into practice in your life are two very different paths.

This is why people all over the world do different forms of relaxation, meditation, and chant. Keeping the mind clear for ten minutes a day can be a very difficult task. Clear means free from all negative thoughts. It's very easy for us to constantly slip back to our comfort zones and never achieve ten minutes of clarity, therefore always remaining desperate. You have to give yourself rules to follow. It's like being a child again, in a way: not eating too many sweets or crying wolf. It's kind of strange, but learning in a way that is not taught to us as children is very difficult. So we have to go right back to the beginning. Most of us actually don't have the first idea of how to reach contentment within ourselves, which in turn gives us clarity of mind, which in turn gives us what we need. This is not our fault, though, as we have all been given others' rules to go by – rules which have come from our parents, from their parents and their parents. Work hard, make money, have a good career, find a wife, have children and pass over. Wouldn't it be so much more valuable to teach us all from birth that love for yourself and others is more important? When you're a small child you don't need for anything – well, just food, love and sleep. It's very different from the way you need as an adult.

It's finding the sanctuary of that past, in your early years, that will open the door for the calmness and feelings of contentment that will give you the ten minutes of free mind that you need each day.

It is so amazing how much we actually know as human beings. It's fascinating, though why we all strive to forget the past and think only what the future holds – what we want and what we need.

4 The inner child

INSTEAD OF LOOKING at different areas of your life, the part we are now entering into takes you that little bit further into just who you are. This is about your life, you in your life. This section is called the inner child because this is the very start of the breaking down process, the point at which your journey begins. This is, if you like, the moment of truth, your time to show to yourself just how brave you are. We are all just living things on this earth, unfortunately for us, our emotional level is that bit more advanced than others. Every now and then, our emotional being needs to be looked at, broken down, and polished.

People often talk about the inner child. When I heard that expression when I was very young, I used to think, "Who are they talking about? Am I like a two-in-one person or something?" Some see the whole incarnation of their inner child, but to a lot of other people it's just some word made up by so-called spiritual people and therapists. This is why this section is included at such an important part of the journey.

Many of us ask ourselves those same questions everyday: "What I am doing here? Who am I?" Those answers are not just there at the click of a finger. It's all about timing. Let's start by talking about how you feel right now.

Pause, think about it for a second or two. The feeling you have right now comes directly from your inner child.

The inner child is like the memory bank, a kind of big vault in which all your thoughts, feelings and emotions are stored.

The idea of being in control of the inner child, to a lot of people, is a scary thing but allowing yourself that chance, in your life, can benefit you so much. The more in touch you are with your inner child the more chance you have at understanding who you are and why you are here. It is essential that you create an emotional foundation for yourself that is strong enough to accept why you are here and for what reasons.

We can live every day and never get close to the knowledge within us. If you take the chance to listen closely to your feelings, they can truly give you so much.

You're probably saying, "That is all well and good, but how can I do this?" The answer is that you've already begun. By reading this book, your emotions are already questioning experiences you've had, whether in your conscious or subconscious. Your journey has begun. You don't have to do anything apart from read, just as though you are staring at a beautiful picture or dreaming about a glorious sunset. Getting to know your inner child isn't going to be a hard type of brave, but instead can be a content type of brave. Understand, the inner child is not a void area of yourself. On the contrary, it is your life force, your engine.

Let's move on to your childhood. You need to honest with yourself right now. Are you someone who has hidden your childhood away? Maybe it's because there was too much pain there. If you're not that person and you were fortunate enough to have had a wonderful childhood, I still want you to read this part as it's for everyone.

Being given or shown love, or not being given or shown love, in our childhood ends up being the direct reflection of who we are today. Why is that some people are very angry, some always defensive, others loners, and so on? This is all down to our childhood. Some of you reading this book right now will be saying, "I already know this." Well, that's fine. But do you see how you can improve within yourself? By looking closer at your childhood. It is amazing the impact your childhood can have on you. Your life might be perfect: good job, great wife, and lovely children. But answer this one question. Do you know who you are? Did you say yes? Wow, you must be some human being! There is always some part of your inner child that needs to be looked at, polished. Your childhood is as good a place as any to start.

Inner Child Exercise

A great way to test yourself to see how far you've come to knowing yourself is to find some old family pictures. Get them out and take a really good look, remembering the event and how you felt, and how that makes you feel today. This is why we talked about being brave. It's so important to be able to look at your younger years with total happiness and give forgiveness to anyone who has brought up anger or sadness.

None of us is perfect and everything just takes time. The reason I'm very confident in what I'm saying is that I experienced things that made me want to look and learn. Let me give you an example. As I explained in the introduction, it was my childhood that moulded in me the need to change. The fact that my childhood was fairly traumatic for me made me look and learn. How thankful I am now, to be able to look back, and learn so much from sadness. It has made me stronger and more aware. It has helped me to deal with life as an adult with more ease. Whatever happens in your childhood, whether it be divorce, abuse, rejection or loneliness, you can learn, learn how to grow and become strong. Do not give up on your past. Let it help you to become whole again.

There's a global understanding that comes with breaking down emotion, especially when it comes to staring the years of childhood in the face. The pictures always work. They conjure up so much emotion in us that we are forced to listen to, and to feel, who we are. But it's all about timing. So don't get the pictures out yet, if you don't feel ready.

Opening up old doors of the past can be harsh. Without the seed there can be no flower. So, without opening the doors you can never grow, which means you will also never know.

Occasionally I like to sit and daydream about my childhood. The more tears that fall, the greater the triumph. For the men reading this, "Big boys don't cry". What a load of rubbish! Tears of sadness, tears of happiness – remember it's all positive.

This is just one of the areas of breaking down yourself. Look right into your soul, breakdown and then rebuild. It seems like quite a long process, doesn't it? Well, for some it might well be, but what an amazing journey we're on together. We are finding out who we really are.

5 Learning to live with change

OFTEN WHEN A PERSON DECIDES to mend their ways or change their perception of life, it can become very difficult to live day-to-day without any kind of structure.

As discussed in the 'inner-child,' emotions can become extremely overwhelming when not carefully and sensitively looked after. As day passes into night and night passes into day we may often become anxious about the changes that are occurring due to our new outlook. It can't be expressed how important it is to not overlook any of the areas mentioned and to manifest as much determination as possible. I don't ever see failure as a possibility when trying to better my outlook on life and therefore would never contemplate closing the doors behind me on what I've learnt and given up. I'm also quite sure that you feel the same way. For many of us change is daunting. When taking a journey of self-discovery change is inescapable. You will not only see changes in yourself, you will also see many changes in everyone around you. This self-discovery is life changing. Self-development is not something you will find in a magazine, or acquire just because you talk to your friends about it. This is the real deal. Have an overhaul, fix up the engine and we'll soon be off.

This may seem to be making one of the most wonderful experiences of your life sound like a fix-up job at your local garage, but that's kind of what we are doing. We are breaking down all the areas of yourself and putting them back together with a fine-tune. The reason such a pure topic of angelic proportion is being related to a car is that many books aren't grounded enough. Do you agree? We want to be able to relate, don't we? Every day, life is changing and with that change our awareness becomes stronger. Therefore, with so much change occurring within us, we need structure.

One of the best ways to deal with change in emotion is to just let it go, simply to feel it and then imagine it like a visual picture and then literally throw it away in your mind.

Letting go Exercise

Remember, something that happened with an old friend or your father or mother when you were younger, whether it be a good or bad experience – bad meaning an opportunity for learning. Close your eyes and feel the thought, rather than just thinking it. If you have managed to achieve this, then this would be reward time. Transforming a thought into a feeling enables you to also transfer it back to a visual image, which, in turn, enables you to throw it away.

The throwing away process is so helpful when you need to keep a clear and balanced mind. With so many changes occurring emotionally, being able to do this will give you room for further development.

The process of breaking down yourself will be a fairly hard process of self-development for anyone. But always remember: change is inevitable. Why wait for you, when you've never been anywhere but right here?

Another area of learning to live with change is sacrificing part of what you once were for the new you. It's kind of like going on a diet or cutting down to three pints of lager rather then ten.

I totally appreciate what self-discovery entails and that you know you want to be a calmer, more balanced person who feels positive and thinks well of others. But I also know we're all only human and that it takes some longer than others to fulfill their emotional goals. Without sacrifice you will be adding years to spiritual development rather than months. You don't have to change your whole life. It is entirely up to you. It's at your pace, and with that will be your choice of where you end up and in what time. It's like anything in life. You live and you learn.

6 Coping with loss

LOSS IS EMOTIONALLY DIFFICULT to deal with in anyone's life. Whether it is loss of a friend, a relationship that has come to an end, loss of a family pet or the most difficult of all, loss of a loved one.

Everyone will have experienced some form of loss in his or her life.

I have experienced loss, loss of loved ones in my family. The loss came at different times in my life and for me it was like a great gust of wind that blew me over. Just getting back up was tough in itself but I learned that, with time, the healing process would give me strength.

The process of grieving changed so much about the way I saw life; it made me feel privileged to have life, in what seemed like a blink of an eye.

In the grieving process, I felt my emotions were on a roller-coaster ride. One minute I was happy, and the next minute I was in floods of tears with great sadness. The immense loss engulfed me.

When we think about those heart-rending times which for many is understandably not very often, it is painful. Most of us cannot bear to look back and remember the way we felt at our time of loss, because loss for many people can take years to overcome. This is why it is important to be able to cope with loss, even if it is just for temporary periods of time.

Loss can become an illness if not dealt with in a sensitive manner and will eventually eat its way through your heart and soul until you feel numb. I know I can't tell anybody to overcome his or her loss and to be brave; I can only try. Be brave. As loss has different degrees of pain, depending on the circumstance, it is important to not become a victim. Instead, embrace loss in all its entirety and ride it like a wave.

If we know we are suffering emotionally from a loss in life, we must face it. If we see a close friend or relative suffering from loss, we must be there for them. Don't judge or push; just be ready to catch them if they fall.

I always found that when I got through the initial period of grieving I became a lot more aware of my emotions and, generally, of myself. The process gave me a sense of knowledge. When the waves of pain rushed over me, I didn't run from them. I faced them. Allow the tears to flow or the anger to rage; it is very important to not block in any of the emotions of loss that need to surface within you.

It doesn't matter who you are in this world, a milkman or the Dalai Lama; when loss hits you, it hits hard and there is really nothing we can do about the process that comes with it. What we can do is prepare ourselves so that when it does arrive, we are that little bit more capable.

Preparation for loss runs in tandem with faith in that the belief you need to have within comes from faith. This is when you need to ask yourself the big questions. Do you believe there is an afterlife? Do you believe there is a God? If you do, whether you're religious or not, it will help you cope much easier with loss.

Loving someone is an incredible gift and no one wants their love to be taken away. So, you can begin by accepting that we are all here for just a short period of time. We can never be 100% prepared for loss, but we can try to see it for what it is. See it in its glory.

Loss is a transitional state of mind; a place where you have to expect the change and have the faith to let go.

Console yourself in knowing that there is an afterlife where our loved ones go when it's their time to leave us.

Another comforting way in which to cope with loss is dreaming. Daydreaming. In fact, do not let anyone tell you that you cannot talk to your loved ones who have left you. Your conscious mind does that enough. Imagine to your heart's content that they are with you at anytime you wish. It is not a wise thing to try to forget your loved ones and move on. Always allow yourself that magical time to remember special moments in life before the passing of loved ones. It is also just as important that when you bring new people into your life they too understand the loss you've experienced, and you theirs. This is because loss can creep up on you at any time and if it's caged in and not left to run its course within your life, it can often cause more pain in the future.

7 Removing the negativity

EARLIER WE TALKED about positivity and its important place within the world. It is now at this point, the beginning of your self-development journey, that you can start to delve much deeper into ways of keeping negativity as far away from your soul as possible.

Negativity is like fire. It rips through the life of every person at some point in his or her existence, bringing with it a trail of destruction and harm that creates huge voids in the lives affected.

To truly understand positivity within yourself, you have to take negativity head-on, right within the burning pain that it causes. This is why people also say something good always comes from something bad. Try the following exercise.

Removing the Negativity Excercise: week 1

Imagine a time when you felt lost or upset, preferably involving someone else. For example, maybe a friendship had finished abruptly due to jealousy. Jealousy is often the main reason for friendships that fall apart. Let the scenario be with someone from your past who is still living on the earth plane. The reason for this is that if you follow all the steps, the friendship will probably flower into a much stronger friendship.

Now imagine the very moment the spark turned into fire and all hell broke loose. You may have been fortunate; it may have ended with the friend not returning your calls. If that was the case, you got off very lightly.

Take a pen and a sheet of paper and sit quietly by yourself. You could be in a car with a friend, at home, on a bus – basically anywhere – while doing this part of the exercise. Now, write the name of the old friend over and over again. Keep writing their name as many times as possible on the piece of paper. If you run out of space, find another sheet. If you run out of paper, wait until you can get some more, later in the same day or even the next.

When you get a spare couple of minutes each day continue to do this remembering how upset you where when the fall-out happened. It is important at this point to remember the sadness, anger or downright frustration you felt so that we can turn the negative into positive. You see, nothing can truly be without the two halves of negative and positive coming together.

By writing your friend's name down over and over again you are creating a direct link to the friend: your old friend, soon again to be new. You are opening up the inner vacuum. The inner vacuum is the space where immediate aspects of the thought process get sucked back and forth from person to person. What is amazing about this is the more you write their name the more their subconscious responds to yours. This is such an important step in your self-development. It brings that part of your past that has been affected by negativity into your present in a positive state. Please refer back to any section you feel necessary if you're losing focus in that area.

Now we move on to the next part of this process. You've written the name down over and over and now are probably sick of the sight of the name. Are you sick of it? Fine, let's move on.

Removing the Negativity Excercise: week 2

Now tear up all the pieces of paper with your friend's name and throw them in the bin. The reason for this is to symbolise that the old friend is gone but your new friend is yet to come, negative-free.

Now, start to imagine a beautiful place, a place where you would love to go. It may be a gorgeous beach, or a very peaceful field, or even a large busy city – wherever suits you. As before, do this wherever you are, whenever you can. Imagine yourself in this dream place and first feel the place around you. Now, imagine your old friend there with you. The two of you are so relaxed, content and happy that neither of you want to be anywhere else. Do this for a week. You can do this exercise wherever you want to; there's no pressure.

After doing this for one week, forget about it completely for another week.

Removing the Negativity Excercise: week 3

At the beginning of the third week, go back in your mind to the place that you chose in the first week. Imagine yourself talking to your friend for the first time. Picture yourself talking to him or her about anything – pure trivial chit-chat. Over the week, the conversation you are having together will grow. This may not seem like self-development, but just wait and see the outcome.

> ## Removing the Negativity Excercise: week 4
>
> You are now at the fourth week – the final week. Now do as you did in the first week: write their name repeatedly on a piece of paper. This time keep the memory of the beautiful place you were both chatting in while you write the name down. Now, forget about this four-week process and see what happens.

Let me say this, people will put the outcome down to coincidence. But let me tell you whatever happens between you and that friend, you must remember it was down to your focus that negativity was turned into positivity and your friendship was reborn, stronger and with fewer flaws.

8 The walls of silence

MOVING ALONG to this next and last section involves the negative and positive feelings that may occur within you if you have taken the step to discovery. When you open your heart and mind to so many untamed emotions that have been locked away for so long, many different outcomes may occur. For many of us, a sense of sadness will overwhelm our very being and create the need for shutdown.

Shutdown is the reaction to a pure emotion that creates a wall of silence around you.

To help you avoid shutdown, imagine that you are surrounded by white light, warm white light, while reading this text. Close your eyes to imagine it if you need to, until you feel settled. This will help.

Emotions can be like never-ending tidal waves flooding over our hearts and souls. This is why we must learn to respect emotion. Be loyal to it when discovering yourself. Do not run from it; if you find that you are trapped in what feels like a wall of silence, no man's land, alone, remember that you are not alone. You will get through this and there is gold at the end of the rainbow. Stay positive!

Shutdown is your indication to you that you have emotions you don't want to face. You must understand that they are all part of the greatest journey you'll ever take. When you start to truly see the greatness that you will achieve and with it the potential within you, you will be amazed. You will feel like you can walk on water, even that you have been reborn. We are not walking this planet to hate and judge but to love and be loved. The closer you get to self-discovery, the closer you'll get to love. Isn't that everyone's real ambition, whether they admit it or not?

When you feel trapped in the walls of silence it is very important not to attack others with your pain. This is something that could very well happen, if you let it. You might find it quite difficult at first to embrace the feelings that you are discovering. Don't worry. No one will judge you. Besides, the most important thing is that you do not judge yourself. Remember this is your choice and your journey. You can share your happiness and pain but only with someone who understands and wants to be there for you.

If at any time you feel you don't have anyone to share your emotional experiences with then just walk with me. Imagine us walking with each other on this beautiful golden road with a rainbow shining in the sky.

If you believe you have a purpose in life then surely you would want to be as emotionally balanced as possible to take on your challenges. Why is it so difficult? Why do we run from what is actually so divine: our selves? What is it about human beings that creates so much fear and shutdown? You could ask those questions forever and a day, and many people will. But many others – one of which may be you – will progress, listen, and have faith in themselves. Do not let the walls of silence lock you in forever.

Isn't it funny how when you go out to parties or to a restaurant, you can always spot someone who is trapped in the silence? It's kind of strange because it's not something that you may actually see in someone, it's more like what you can feel in someone. If you have experienced that, how do you feel? Does it make you feel a bit uncomfortable? If it doesn't then, hey, you have no heart. (Only joking!) It is just one small example of a social situation where someone hasn't controlled and respected their emotions. Instead, their emotions have become like rockets firing all over the place.

We must walk before we run, if only step by step we come.

Self-discovery can become like a drug, the thirst for personal growth. Be very aware of this as it can become addictive. Remember: step by step!

> ### Tip
>
> A great little tip if you've found yourself feeling trapped is to totally distract yourself from the very moment you feel your emotions racing out of control. Do something different. Go into another room, turn on the television, or put some music on. Basically, do anything else but what you are doing. However, do not phone a friend.

At this point it's about managing your own emotions. Remember, breaking down yourself to create a better you is called that for a reason. As soon as you feel calm, after the wave of emotion has passed, write down all you've felt. It is always good to keep notes on your feelings. I keep my own diary of emotions, which I separate into different parts; one part for good days and one for bad. It really does come in handy when trying to connect emotions to certain events.

Sometimes I think how great it would be to be given a little magical handbook that gives us all our balanced emotions. But then I suppose if we had that we wouldn't get such blissful rewards or those feelings that ooze all over your body when you know you have achieved something.

A point that is necessary to make at this place within your self-discovery is reward. Give yourself personal rewards at any point when you feel you have broken new ground. Obviously, don't go rewarding yourself just because you can tell the next-door neighbour's dog you love it. Be realistic. On a more serious note, time is always a healer. You are not alone in this quest for a better life and you know that deep down inside you can't go wrong. Finding ways to better yourself and rewarding yourself when you achieve your goals has always been great therapy, a spiritual therapy that is. Just knowing that you've even bought a book like this, and that you are reading it, is a major breakthrough. Too many people talk about their self-discovery, their spiritual courses and their revelations. What it's really all about is getting down to the nitty-gritty of yourself. Get stuck in. Go through the emotions and do not give in. The walls of silence will always be there. All you have to do is keep working, keep searching. Find the key to the door in the wall, walk the rainbow road and find the gold. Keep on reading and step by step we'll do it together.

Realisation: making your mind work for you

4

1 The here and now

THE LAST THREE CHAPTERS should have given you the desire to do something for yourself, to change the way you live your life and to create a better present and a brighter future for yourself. Remember: do not give in.

So far you've been given the basic tools necessary to have an overview of different areas to be aware of in life. Some people view spiritual development with flippancy. They often feel there's no need to put in the groundwork, preferring to just jump to their place of peace and wisdom. Sorry, folks. That's just not possible.

We need to address fundamental issues within ourselves to achieve a clearer understanding and to reach the goal of spiritual development. It is also imperative that we look into the subjects listed previously with our feet firmly on the ground by remaining in the present, the here and now.

Living in the here and now means that you are aware of your past and are ready to await whatever comes to you from the future. As we take the journey within the book to much greater meanings and spiritual levels, it is very important that to get there we understand about being in the here and now.

Treat previous passages as your notebook on getting started and to help you stay focused on the right things rather then the wrong. It all adds up to a great part of you, the part that your conscious and subconscious deals with every day. Another reason why it is so important to live in the here and now is that you won't get stuck in the past. Dwelling on regrets or what you should or should not have done is futile. There is simply no time for regrets or feeling sorry for yourself. You have to stay positive as much as you can whether you are looking at the inner child or you are coping with loss or betrayal. It can be very hard on the heart, but briefly looking at what may be the wrongs in your life and not dwelling on them is the only way to make them right.

It can be very difficult to live in the here and now, which is why it is necessary to discuss it.

Most of us in life will at some point find it nearly impossible to just stay in today's thoughts. As you've been reading now, how many times has your mind popped into the future? Did you think about having to take your children to school? What you will eat for dinner? Or whether or not you've done the ironing? You see it takes a lot of practice to get the conscious mind tuned into a way that helps you to stay centred.

Centring yourself is about focus and concentration. Concentrate on not wanting to know about tomorrow and not wanting to know about yesterday. It might seem a bit basic to a lot of you, but it works.

Here and Now Exercise

A great way to achieve the here and now is to focus on something you need to do today that you have been meaning to do, and stick to it. By doing this, you will find that you have more and more things that need to be done today rather than tomorrow. It gets your mind thinking in the right way.

Without the mind taking control of the actions, can we control our day-to-day thoughts? The more you do actual, physical things in your day that are for that day, the more you will start to feel grounded and centred. You know what it's like when you haven't finished work that needs to be done, or you can't get around to making time for it because you're spending too much time thinking about the future. Remember that today is today and tomorrow is tomorrow. Think of it this way, you wouldn't want to pay a bill today that didn't need to be paid until tomorrow, would you? Once you have started to train yourself to stick to the duties of the day your subconscious mind will kick in and act as a kind of alarm clock to your conscious mind, reminding you that if you start wandering back into the past or dwelling on the future, the bells will ring in your mind and alert you to needing to re-centre yourself.

It can be a real challenge to master this kind of mind control. It leaves others standing when it comes to being able to take the here and now on board and learn about yourself. If you don't, you'll end up all mixed up, confused and anxious, wishing you'd never decided to become a better person.

Another point to add is that it doesn't matter where you are within your journey or how far you've travelled, what you've managed to address in yourself, or even what you feel you cannot master. When you read back over the passages, which you will do because they won't stop niggling you until you've mastered them, you will see a picture building up of yourself. The picture will be different for everyone; but whatever you feel, go with it. Don't let anyone tell you that you are wrong in what you feel, or that the decisions you are making are not the right ones. Always remember that this journey you are taking, this picture of self-discovery is painted especially for you, by you. You've looked at the pain, seen how you'll gain, now let your mind take control and weather the rain. The best place to be is here. The best time to be here is now.

2 Working with the subconscious

THE SUBCONSCIOUS PART of your mind is undoubtedly the most powerful part of your working mind. It delivers information to your conscious mind twenty-four hours a day. It not only helps to run your body, but also to constantly help you see the right way in which to improve your life. The trick is that you have to listen to what your subconscious is trying to tell you. The subconscious is the father of all fathers, our own personal guru. It is the guru's wisdom on tap. Huh! If only it was that easy.

Making sure that you don't block out what your subconscious is trying to tell you is probably your most difficult challenge.

You see, listening to your subconscious and hearing what it is saying to you is hard. But hearing what it is saying and doing something about it... well, they are two very different things.

Your subconscious plays the largest part of all in self-development. Every single guru, Dalai Lama, or wise human being walking this earth doesn't give what he or she reads from a book. They give what they feel, deep within their subconscious.

When we think in our conscious minds we are constantly cross-examining our subconscious. The most amazing thing of all is that if you grow to love yourself by being positive, you will be more able to learn from your subconscious. Put in the groundwork and reap the rewards.

Psychologists, therapists, doctors and scientists have all had major discussions about the subconscious. They all question its power and ability. Do we really have the ability to channel other times or to have the ability to read another mind? You can have exactly what you wish regarding the subconscious mind as long as you believe.

Believing in what you hear within yourself is a killer test. You know what you must do, but do you do it?

I've talked to so many people that have just as much spiritual potential as the next person but for some reason can't seem to get their belief system into gear.

Not listening to the subconscious is why so many lives are in ruin, financially and emotionally. We can strive to become the image of perfection, but only if we listen to the true direction. You can see how important the relationship between the conscious and subconscious mind is. All your worries and fears of life described in the previous chapters are more often than not, stored in the subconscious. Therefore, the more you learn to listen to what your subconscious is saying the easier it will become for you to master it. You will see a picture building up of yourself. The picture will be emotions that appear from nowhere. Listening to your subconscious, and being in control of it, is like unlocking the door to internal wisdom, reading the signs given and then closing it afterwards. It's a great way to live your life.

You must also remember that the conscious mind only works in a relative sense; it can only help you with what you have already given to it. It's only there for your entire relative day-to-day needs. It too can help you answer questions, but often the answers you get back are untrue, slightly twisted and misguided because your conscious mind can only answer from knowledge of experience, whereas the subconscious is able to work all by itself with no alter egos to sway the outcome. Learning to work with your subconscious will be so beneficial to you in every part of your life that you won't be able to live without it.

There are many unanswered questions regarding the subconscious. One of them is, why do we dream?

And, what are our dreams trying to tell us? Could it be possible that our dreams are an insight into decisions that need to be made in our lives? Or are they just images that are feelings turned to visuals for no other reason than to sleep? These questions have baffled scientists for years.

Personally, I believe they have a direct relationship to our relative lives in our waking state.

Tip 1

The greatest way to see what they mean is to always write down what you remember about your dreams and log the changes day-to-day.

The subconscious is so powerful. It works purely of its own accord and that it gives preconceived messages to our conscious mind for us to work out and learn.

Tip 2

Keep a log of your dreams and believe in the very first thing that comes to mind, or that first feeling you have that's deep inside, when asking for the answer. Don't let your conscious mind dictate what it thinks the dream means, as your own life experience may jeopardise the outcome.

Every day, people are learning more about dreams within the subconscious and are coming up with all sorts of scientific reasons. When dealing with dreams, listen only to yourself. It is you that comes into this world alone, and you that leaves alone.

Subconscious Mind Exercise

When working with your subconscious a very simple test is this: think of a question about your life, a question that's about something not too far into the future. For example, just ask yourself the question in your mind: "Am I going to get that new job I've just had an interview for?" "Will I win anything in the next three weeks?" Keep it simple. When you ask the questions, try to feel the answer in your conscious mind. Do not think about it or wait to try to get an answer. If the answer does come from your subconscious, it will be instant.

continued...

> *...continued*
>
> If you get an instant answer, try asking the question for a total of four times. If your mind is calm and you are thinking clearly you should feel the same answer each time. If you do not get the answer, have faith. Do not doubt, no matter what, and wait for the outcome.

Remember, your subconscious is a very powerful tool. If it is not used correctly, it will not do the job. Lose faith in your subconscious and it will have no choice but to lose faith in you. Belief is the key. Let your subconscious tell the truths and your conscious be the proof.

For many people, as it was for myself at the beginning, understanding why we need to be aware of our subconscious and conscious minds was quite difficult at the time, not to mention frustrating. I used to question: "How can my subconscious be able to have any affect on my life, without any real proof? Apart from my dreams, how do I know it even exists?"

When I was about ten years old, I first heard of the phenomena called the near-death experience. I was very curious to find out more about it. If somebody has been pronounced dead, which means that their brain has stopped working, then how do they explain walking into the white light or so many of the other unexplained subconscious phenomena of the near-death experience? If that's not something to do with the subconscious, then what is it? And if so, where else can it take us? These are all such wonderful and fascinating questions that can only be answered by the subconscious mind. If you don't feel ready to work the subconscious part of your mind, don't worry. It's all about timing. It will be your time when it's supposed to be. Maybe you have to concentrate on betrayal. Who knows? Whatever will be, will be. It's in your hands.

3 Living without doubt

SOMETIMES YOU ARE GOING TO FEEL OVERWHELMED by so much information. Sometimes you are going to feel that to continue your quest for a better spiritual life you'll have to give in and try another day. You'll sometimes feel that this can't be a journey that you can conquer and that you are too vulnerable to change. Never forget the purpose of what you are trying to achieve. Try to remember why you decided to go on a quest for a better you, and always give yourself time to stop and do nothing. It is very important that you do not overcrowd your mind with so much information that it all becomes a blur.

The whole purpose for writing this book in small easy-to-read passages, is so that you can always skip back to any part of the journey when you feel you've forgotten a part that's key to you. The reason many people fall from their path is that they panic at the first sight of difficulty. You have to stay focused and grounded within yourself for long as possible within your day-to-day life.

When looking at the separate passages of information, spend a fair amount of time thinking about what has been written, rather then rushing to get to the bit you feel is more relevant to you. The whole journey is relevant. The only way to live without doubt within your conscious and subconscious is to believe. This is why it is so important to know where you're at in your spiritual self, and not to believe you're somewhere that you're not. Without first getting together the whole picture of information, breaking it down then putting it back together, can you achieve your goal .You first have to fight in a war to know what it's like to survive a war.

The only time you will doubt yourself is when you let yourself get dragged down by the lack of belief in your purpose or in your journey, or when you let others do it for you.

No matter what age you are or where you are going in life, there will always be people trying their best to bring you down, to make you feel bad about yourself or to make you doubt your very existence. If you haven't found your true spiritual vocation, it makes it even harder to fend off these unwanted negativities.

When you watch a movie about martial arts, there's usually a wise old spiritual master who understands all and that no one can ever hurt. Of course he could be hurt physically, but this is not necessarily the point they're trying to make. The image of his power in physical strength, together with the image of his spiritual and mental strength, seems to make him the untouchable one. Not only is he really tough, but he is also very popular. Why? It's because people are always drawn to a person who is mentally balanced and physically fit. You don't have to be Bruce Lee to find yourself. The more you believe in the power you have within you, the less you will doubt yourself. Therefore, without having to be egotistical with it, you will be more attractive to others. The more other people like, love and respect you, the more you respect the power within yourself. Why change that? If it's working for you, go for it.

Real life is no movie when it comes down to it. The test of personalities in the real world is a lot harder. But once again, it's about your belief and lack of doubting. You will have to be very patient with yourself and with others around you. As you can imagine, not everyone is walking a path of self-discovery, so it's important not to shout out about your new-found wisdom as it might put people off.

Finding your mental balance to create an air of calm is also very important in living without doubt. In the Bruce Lee movies, it's his ability to maintain a constant focus of calm and tranquility that makes him attractive to others. The power of the mind is the key to the power of the body and total belief.

A great way of achieving a steady positive mental balance is by using your conscious mind to gain control over a negative situation. The majority of time in life where you are going to feel in doubt of yourself will be when you are around others. The worst time for fear or doubt is when there is a lot of alcohol being consumed. Alcohol will create a kind of dirty film across your mind that disables you from seeing things clearly. Therefore, you misjudge others. Try to keep yourself away from drunken states when trying out this test.

Living Without Doubt Exercise

If you find yourself in a negative conversation with anyone, a friend, a partner, a colleague or even a stranger, remember the following statement: living without doubt. Keep it going round in your mind while listening to the other person's comments. Every time the other person says something negative in a question try to answer them back in the best positive manner possible. If they are talking generally about something or someone in a negative manner, try to add as many positive points into the conversation as possible.

Not only will doing this make you feel a lot better about yourself, you will also feel more powerful like the wise old martial arts master. It will also help to train your mind to create a more positive outlook within you, and in turn you will appear calm and powerful. People will feel no need to doubt you and this will make you much more attractive to them, which in turn will make you feel very happy, with no reason to doubt yourself. Once you've started to create this kind of mental action more often than not you will start to achieve positive power where ever you go, and in turn will make your doubt go to give you space to grow.

4 Living for proof

MANY OF US dare not believe that there possibly exists something so wonderful that it could change our life around, unless it was a million pounds. Don't get me wrong. I don't think money is bad, but money can only buy you things, not true spiritual clarity.

If you spend your whole life forcing the issue of proof, it will never ever come. If you find yourself questioning someone that has something to offer that is not material, how will you ever change? Life is amazing. We are lucky to have been given the opportunity to see the wonderful things we see and to feel the beautiful feelings inside us.

At first it felt strange including a passage about proof but even though we all want to believe something and we all want to find the truth, we do need proof. Be warned: wanting and needing proof can be a dangerous game of cat and mouse. If you spend your entire time judging or looking for something that doesn't exist, more often than not you've missed the point. It all boils down to the belief factor. You might just be that person who is questioning every single thing that is written in this book. Now, that is great news, because you are exactly the person who can be helped to better your spiritual outlook.

You may have read about love and faith and karma, and passed on that. Well, here is news for you. If you want to walk a road to spiritual discovery, you have to put the groundwork in. If you go around like a headless chicken searching for an answer that you won't find externally because it only lives internally, you need to feel that you are also very able to change, to become empowered within your own positive state of mind. You need to know deep down inside that you are not alone and that if you feel vulnerable or afraid then you can use this book to comfort yourself. There are millions of people all around the world feeling exactly like you: can't change, want to change, but won't change because can't change. Everybody can change, and as you read this book you are changing. That is your proof, you don't know it yet, but you will by the time you have finished the book. At this point it maybe very hard to see the connection between yourself and the passages, but it will come in time. Even if you're still searching at the end of the book, that's OK. Just ask yourself this: if you've always been looking for proof, then why is it that you can't see that you are the proof? It's you that has bought the book; it's you that is reading it. Look no further. The only proof you need is that you are able to change. Hey, look what's happening right now!

If you have understood what you have just read, then it's relevant and important that we talk about trust.

Trust in yourself.

Trust that you do not have to fear your journey disappearing. You have already found proof in yourself, by reading this book. The fact that you've seen proof means it can only grow from here. It doesn't matter if you don't live, eat, sleep or breathe spirituality at this early stage. You must give yourself breathing space.

Also, ask yourself why you may worry about losing the trust that you have gained within your own proof. The need for proof is simply just a reflection of the fear deep within. You are the living proof; don't let the fear win.

5 Knowing a good thing

ANOTHER POINT IS, why is it that when something great comes along do we turn on the self-destruct button and totally ruin it?

Knowing a good thing and seeing a good thing for what it is are two very different comparisons. It's easy to know that your girlfriend or husband or flat-mate cooks you fantastic meals every night after work. But it is not so easy to truly see the attentiveness and support for you that is going into doing such a thing. Then wham-bam. It happens. You're having an argument. What's it about? It's about being taken for granted.

This might not seem like on important part of self-development, but it is. Learning to see how important love and support are when given from others plays a big part in your journey. It takes time, but it gives you an opportunity to free your mind of selfishness.

When others spend quality time showing us how they care, whether it be just a friendship or a full-blown romantic relationship. It's not up to them to inform us to how to be grateful, even if they are totally giving. It's up to us to have the good will and sensitivity to see that we have something good right here, right now. Learn to appreciate others in your life. This is a great way to help maintain your balanced mind.

Often, we find ourselves blessed in some way or another with unusual talents, and often find it very difficult to learn how to appreciate them. Whatever it is that you are good at, it does no harm to share what you have with others. Of course, knowing you have a good thing can at times become difficult to see when you have it. But it's about always being aware of your good fortune. Being aware that what you have materially or spiritually may not mean that much to you, but it may be the most magical of dreams to somebody else. So many people hide their talents and gifts away, with no wish to share them with the world. That is their own right, of course, but it is all about either ego or their fear of rejection. It is so important to see that as quickly as you have something in your life, it can be taken from you. If it's God's wish to test you in such a way, then so be it. Understand that to have and to own the smallest of material objects, to breathe the air we are given, or to smell a flower, to not have to live in a world where we have no water or food, is a blessing. People take, take, take in this life and that creates such sadness in the world. Change is the only way forward. People need to take responsibility for their actions and become selfless enough to be thankful for what they have. We can all get sucked into moaning every now and then, but doesn't it really get on your nerves when you see someone sitting at a table pushing food and wine into their face and saying, "I'm broke," when there are millions of people starving in the world? Or, what about people who would rather take their money to the grave than give to a deserving charity for starving and homeless children. People just don't know when they're on to a good thing.

If nothing else, this book aims to inspire people to change. Be part of that positive energy and look at how you're running your life, thankful to others. Make a difference in the way others see you. Be brave and, last but not least, do not be afraid to change. Good things don't always last.

6 Turning knowledge into wisdom

AS YOU READ THIS BOOK page by page, you will be encountering a great deal of thought and with that thought you will be collecting a great deal of knowledge: some you may feel you're already aware of, some you may be just learning now. There are many reasons why it is necessary to give you smaller amounts of information per section. One of them is so that you can get a kind of injection of knowledge: sharp, sometimes a bit painful, but quick. Doing this allows you to learn, understand and then do.

Turn knowledge into wisdom in your day-to-day life, making use of that wonderful brain of yours. For example, take working with your subconscious. The thoughts you have from the time you sleep through to the following day will start to coincide with each other. The more you use the mental abilities that you have, the greater level of brainpower is used. The thing is, how do we turn that extra brainpower and knowledge into something we can deem as tangible wisdom? Simply by taking what is written and putting it into practice. From the moment you transcend from theory to practice it becomes relative. You naturally become wiser. You don't need to act out everything that you read.

What we do and what we say will directly influence the future. Every action has a reaction. Every word has consequence. Therefore, the more knowledge you have to turn into wisdom, the better off you'll be. Try not to speed-read this book as you may miss something.

The more you start to widen your senses and abilities within the realm of spirituality, the more free you will feel and the more at peace you will become. Putting theory into practice will become easier and, in doing so, much more will be achieved.

We need an overall spiritual wisdom to be taught in schools and colleges, not any type of religion, but one of self-belief and spiritual clarity. The more that people put knowledge into action to create wisdom, the closer we get to a brighter new world; a world where we can all have a lot more freedom to speak our minds. In a positive spiritual way, to create a universal goal that can be conquered by positive spirituality. People talk of spiritual revolutions, but it's just talk. What we need is action. You have to ask yourself where you wish to be ten years from now. In a world full of corruption, violence and depravity? Or would you rather work towards a picture of clarity, where people can still do all the things they always have, but do it with peace, respect and love?

We can all become so much wiser by becoming active in our knowledge. Action plays such a major part in making your mind work for you because you are fuelling your wants and needs without wanting and needing. If you try a little bit harder to forgive, or really work at controlling your jealousy, you can be ready for anything. There will be no bridge you can't cross. There will be no mountain too high to climb and no challenge too hard for you to tackle. But, in order to take on the responsibility of being a truly aware, spiritually clear-minded individual, you must start to turn your knowledge into wisdom. Without it, this book can't help you. It can only give you what I give. From that point on it is in your hands. This book will never give you all the answers. If it did, where would you go from here? Every single person who decides to take this spiritual journey takes it in his or her own individual way. You may see the knowledge given very differently to someone else. You may be a quick or slow learner. Take every step in your own time, only when you feel ready. If you feel ready, then explore your spiritual side to your heart's content. But only do it when you are prepared.

Wisdom has no time; it just is.

7 Confronting control

IN THIS SECTION we will talk about control. The issue that affects many, many people is the fear of losing control. Many people cannot admit that they suffer from the fear of losing control. It may be very difficult to admit to. That's because, like many fears, control runs alongside denial. A lot of people find it is so hard to admit that they are control freaks, even to the point of trying to control the words in this passage, so as to avoid changing.

It's definitely the greatest fear in us that forces us as human beings to want to control everything and anything we can. At the end of the day control will only be damaging to ourselves or anything or anyone in its path.

You need to ask yourself, if you are ready to, "Do I try to control others? Do I control others and don't even realise I'm doing it?" You need to be very aware of where you are at with this issue, if at all.

If you are controlling everything in sight, then it's very important to let someone you deeply trust help you. You won't be able to find a way of conquering control with strangers or an acquaintance. You have to do it with a friend.

The fear of losing control most probably comes from a particular period in your childhood. Anyone who has parents, or sisters or brothers, or friends – or anyone for that matter – forcing controlling situations upon them, no matter how small, will probably have suffered some kind of damaging effect, creating a mirror image in their adult life. As we grow into our teenage years, we often rebel or become completely introverted. Then, as we progress into our twenties and upwards, we start to build a life for ourselves. Life continues to grow and flourish, financially and materially. We become adults. We then feel that we need to control our domain for fear of losing control, the control that we most likely used to get us where we are. The issue of control can appear in people at many different stages in their lives, from childhood through to old age. It all depends on whether they feel threatened and at what time. This is why it's very important to seek help from somebody you trust implicitly, and who knows you well.

The first reason for having to know and trust the person is that you will open yourself completely to them emotionally. You must first make sure you are ready to lay your emotional cards on the table before doing so. Secondly, because you have to let your friend judge when they think you are being controlling, to let them stop you in your tracks and ask you to please stop controlling the issue or situation at hand. The third reason is because you have to be sure that there is strict confidence between the two of you. This is for your benefit. Be sure you can trust your friend with your deepest fears.

A very close friend is a great support for getting over the issue of control because it's all about the support that you didn't have when you yourself were being controlled. Therapy is also a good way to working with the issue, but it may be difficult when you find yourself dealing with a total stranger.

Control Exercise

If you have found your person to work with on this issue then you've made a great start. The issue of control is an incredibly in-depth issue and can take a long time to overcome. Each time you are stopped in your tracks by your friend, make a mental note of how you were feeling at that moment. Work out in your mind why it was that you felt you had to control what was happening around you. Keep working on this until you can build up a mental picture of who you might be from an external point view. You can only achieve this by being truly honest with your friend *continued...*

...continued

and with yourself. Connect your mental picture to a time in your life. It may be a time that you have chosen to forget. If so, just try that little bit harder to deal with the emotions that surround the image. Develop an image of forgiveness between what's happening now, and what happened in the past.

See the person or persons in question, no matter how trivial the situation, as helpless – so helpless that they had to control you because that's all they knew. Be aware not only of their facial expressions and tone of voice, but also of any significant smells or images, etc. Remember to relate the present situation to those in the past. The aim here is to see the pain in the other person or people of the past and to feel sorry for them. Once you've achieved that mentally, you can identify the same feelings within yourself, and how embarrassed you are that people may be feeling sorry for you. They can see that you are so afraid of losing control that you have to control everything. It can be a tricky issue to deal with because recognising that you are doing exactly the same as the person or people you most probably grew to hate is a hard feeling to deal with, whoever you are.

If you find yourself happy to leave the control to someone else, then that's fantastic. You must realise that you were never ever really in control. It was the past that was controlling you.

Control is one of the worst issues to come up against. It makes you feel annoyed and frustrated when others are trying to control you. It makes you want to run a mile. Unfortunately the controller often has little or no knowledge about what they are trying to control. That's a special trait of control freaks. They spend so much time trying to control everything around them that they actually end up misjudging and misunderstanding facts about what they are trying to control. So, to us, the person being controlled, it can become totally frustrating. So you see, it is very important to work really hard to become free of fear within control, and to find a way to be content and happy within yourself.

8 The awakening of truth

THE AWAKENING IS THE TIME when you realise that you no longer need to fear the pain of the past, the present or the future. It is the time in which you become reborn – reborn into the new you – wiser and purer. You can learn to forgive and forget and appreciate pain and loss in this most positive form. The awakening brings you that much closer to your true self. Exciting, isn't it? For some it may take as long as it takes them to read this book. For others it may take a lifetime. Not to beat around the bush, opening the door to your higher self is the only answer.

It may be difficult to be truthful with others if they are not walking a journey of self-discovery, and it's likely that they will become defensive or repudiate. Remain truthful to your self at all times.

When you wish for a purer, more spiritual way of life you become aware that without first achieving the basic steps you won't be able to move on to the next. Therefore, the need for you to trust yourself should become a non-issue.

Having an awakening is an unbelievable experience. The time before the awakening is as if you are dead or asleep or in a state of coma. Once you have awoken, you see no negativity, you see nothing as a problem and no challenge too tough. You see, it's all about the mind and the way you look at things. Is your glass half empty or half full? It's all about how you look at it.

Having experienced an awakening you will want to learn more and more about the positive power within yourself. Take your journey slowly, for if you walk too fast you might miss something.

There are many benefits in searching for a greater truth in your being. It isn't just about keeping a more balanced existence. It can also be very beneficial at home. Many of you reading this book will have families of your own. Awakening within yourself can give you such a clearer perception of the needs of your wife or husband or children. You will find yourself feeling more of what they feel rather than feeling alien to their deepest thoughts. An awakening gives you a sense of clearing out the old to make way for the new you.

When I had my awakening to a more spiritual outlook it helped me to understand the importance of respect that I had to give to all areas of life. I saw love in a totally different way. I didn't just see it in my friends or family or partner. I saw it in total strangers and in animals. It became more and more apparent to me just how important love was, and that if I didn't show love to others, and let others show love back to me, that I would be walking the earth the wrong way. It helped me to see all the riches in pain and sadness, showing me all the positive ways in understanding that to sacrifice is to gain for a greater good. There is not a single man or woman or child walking this planet who could persuade me to change the person I am now. I am thankful for the dispirited times in my life, but also grateful to have had the chance to awaken. I really feel it's time for the human race to start taking responsibility for itself and to start learning the steps of an awakening.

I need it; you need it; we all need it, spirituality.

A. B. C.

A S WE ARE NOW about to enter into the second half of the book and onto Step Five, it's an appropriate time to discuss your staying power and dedication to yourself.

It may seem fairly obvious to many of you who are reading this book why we've talked so much about the fundamental human 'do and don't' issues within the first half. For many of you it may not; it may have either not registered with you or you may just be wanting to skip from A to C, without truly learning and understanding B.

You want success from this book and from yourself, correct? OK. If you do, it's best to follow the guidelines at all times. But, at the same time, you can be a winner and achieve your own spiritual potential.

If any of the issues discussed in steps one to four are a direct reflection of an issue that resides within you, you must address it. If you don't address the B issues, it is highly likely that you will never reach C.

If you imagine this journey as a car, you will know that the engine cannot run without fuel, the brakes cannot work without a brake pedal, and you cannot steer without a steering wheel. All the individual parts by themselves are often useless but when they're put together they create the perfect vehicle. You have to understand what has been written and why. It's OK reading something and putting it back on the shelf, but if you don't understand what the words are trying to say, well, that's when it's time to pick up the book once more. These words are for you so that you can build your foundation and move forward to the next part of your journey. If you feel confused about something written within steps one through to four that relates directly to you, then go back and read the relevant section again.

Be honest with yourself and know that you fully understand the areas discussed in the first four steps. Many of you will have understood and will be ready to venture into the next part of your journey. Just check with yourself once again to be sure that you are not hiding yourself behind any denial issues within any of the steps.

How easy life would be if we could just jump from A to C without first understanding B. But how dangerous that would be, for if you try to become the warrior of life, you must be sure your sword is razor-sharp. Without that you would walk a path blind.

This shouldn't be a book that you rush through, wanting to see what comes next, hoping that the magical answer lies on the last page – because it doesn't. The magic lies within the whole book, and can only be seen when you too see the magic. At times it all seems a bit serious. But it doesn't have to be, as long as you listen to the words as well as read them. See it as a journey, and you will start to feel different feelings within your body and mind that will excite you to who you are going to become.

There is no doubt that every one of you reading this book will achieve your own spiritual awakening because you want to learn how to become better people. This book is made for believers; the human beings of tomorrow; the spiritual directors of their own lives. This book is about carrying a message to everyone who reads it, so they can then pass that message on; the message of spiritual freedom – individual spiritual freedom. If you believe, and wish to become the spiritual director of your own life, then you must now read on, for the next four steps take you further into yourself, further into your higher self. Let yourself be guided through life by you, the wisdom and the words.

Seeing is about believing and where we are going to go with the second half of the book. Steps five to eight are all about the practice of spirituality, the preparation, the knowledge and the action.

You have sowed the seeds in steps one to four. Understanding the fundamental issues of our existence, the roots of our tree. Now it is time to build on that knowledge you have taken on board. People talk about being spiritual, "I'm spiritual because I've read some books." That is not necessarily the case. You can gain knowledge from reading books, but only by putting the words you read into practice in your everyday life can you truly become a spiritual person.

Steps five to eight give you the insight into doing the spiritual work needed to reach a higher spiritual plane within yourself. The words talk of the ancient art of channelling, protecting ourselves from negative energies, understanding that we are a modern society and that we are ready for a spiritual breakthrough; the process of practising the art of spirituality through meditation, learning to do as the American Indians do and speak with our spiritual guides, and much, much more.

Steps five to eight are the most exciting steps because they let you know that you are ready to try to become that new you. You have sowed the seeds in the first half of the book; now it's time to water them so that by the time you've finished the book you can start to watch them grow. Remember that finding your true spiritual potential can often take longer for some than for others. You always have to allow yourself time to become aware. Be graceful in your approach to practising the art of spirituality. Do not force any of the issues with regards to channelling etc. These gifts, when they show themselves to you fully, are very powerful but also very precious. It is important not to abuse them, and to be thankful for whatever stage you find yourself getting to.

Good luck!

The preparation for your spiritual transition: the vision begins

1 Moving with the times

THIS IS WHERE WE'RE AT: the age of the millennium. We are no longer living in the Stone Age. There are many of you out there that are constantly in fear of being mocked for being spiritual. Yes, there is a time and place for spiritual chit-chat, but as we grow into our new skin, so we must pull together and move with the times.

There are many more people in the world finding themselves forever getting nearer and nearer to the need for spiritual enlightenment, most for the right reasons; some for the wrong reasons.

Even at this early stage that you are at now, you are learning and understanding. You will be attracting like-minded people without even knowing it, finding that, at the most bizarre moments, the conversations you're having will find themselves in the land of spirituality. When this happens, be aware but be available. Find out what others' views are and see how they differ from yours. In doing this you will start to understand what your true beliefs are. You will start to feel that much stronger in your belief of yourself because when you are walking this true spiritual path, free from religious limitations, you will find that you will always come across people with totally different beliefs. Often, they are forceful in their beliefs. For you, it is about listening, observing, and understanding who and what you don't want to be. When this happens in your day-to-day life it will start to confirm your journey, symbolised by this book. You will start to see that you are already moving with the times. If you can rid yourself of the fears that hold most people on this earth back, then you have already moved on. This is a sign that you are becoming a spiritual director of your own life.

It will be hard for some of you at first because you may have been part of a religion from birth, but preparing for your journey is about moving with the times, because the journey is of truth and the truth always survives. You do not necessarily have to release your belief in the religion that holds you. Just be honest with yourself, and start moving with the times. There is no place in the new spiritual revolution that is approaching for Stone Age views.

Equal opportunity encourages everyone to have an opinion on any given subject. But the words of truth are only about one thing and given for only one reason: for you to grow. There is much scripture written as though it's written to cage the reader rather than set them free. We are forever moving forwards and, with that, creating a new spiritual outlook. At times, for many it can create panic because change within belief can be foreseen as an evil transition. But if you truly look into your heart about many words that have been written to guide us in our lives, can you honestly say you feel a sense of trust, belief or even faith in what you have read? For so many years we have lived as if we are frozen in time, with many people on the earth holding on as tightly as they can to what is left of religion as we know it. It is an incredibly sad time for many honest and caring people with pure hearts. It just may be too late for them. Sometimes certain religions can create a smokescreen to truth and therefore any person or people living in faith of that religion will never sway. But what I am talking about is not religion. It's just you, me, us, – everyone; everyone pulling together to create a unified spirituality that is individual to each and every person. It's a choice that we all have within our paths of life whereby we can share our new-found wisdom or can keep it locked away within ourselves. Either way is fine as you can't tell someone what to say or do when talking of their faith. You can't make people change their ways of faith. You can just open a door and let them walk through it, as you are doing right now as you read this book: moving with the times.

2 Learning to fight the vampires of spirituality

THE MORE YOU GROW WITHIN YOURSELF on this journey, the more vulnerable you also become. Vulnerable in that you have started to obtain something within you that people will wish to ridicule: belief. These people are the vampires of spirituality. It's amazing because whenever your energy levels rise in a positive vibration, so you become more attractive and start to create a magnetism around yourself. There will always be a vampire of spirituality somewhere, just waiting to break you down – and more often than not, in front of others, because this is how they get their kicks. It's a kind of fight between good and evil. As soon as the evil of the world hears that you are training to become a new warrior of good, the evil energy sends its soldiers out to war – the war of good and evil.

Even at the early stage you are at, understanding and wishing to learn about love and karma, etc., you have started the ball rolling. The more you learn and understand, the more powerful you become, powerful in wisdom and positivity. This is something that spiritually evolved people notice. As soon as you start to achieve certain steps of self-discovery, it seems as though you automatically open doors to different energies, negative as well as positive. No one has been able to explain this and only the most positively powerful spiritual human beings will recognise the significance of the two: good and evil. As long as there is good there will always be evil. It has always seemed to be that when you're on your spiritual journey you are given tests; tests that seem to come not from any one person, but from the universe itself. The closer you get to finding the truth of pure spiritual enlightenment, the harder the tests become.

This is why it's so important to be aware of any vampires of spirituality trying to suck away your good energy replacing it with bad.

An example of how they can easily get to you is through social situations. Most people like to have a drink and party, but in doing so they lower their energy levels and decrease the level of positive power available to them. The more alcohol you consume, the less you are aware, aware of who is about to pounce on you. There is obviously a real concern for drugs within the realm of the vampires. The higher the level of drug the more vulnerable you are to all kinds of deviant harm. The whole idea of turning from dead-in-the-water zombie to human soul to highly sensitive powerful spiritual human being is that you maintain a consistency with it. No one is saying that you can't go to the pub for a drink with your friends or go out clubbing, but just be very aware of who is surrounding you. Like I said earlier, as you become more aware, you open doors to many other energies. You have to also be able to control yourself when it comes to physical attraction because, as you change within yourself, you can often become more able to communicate as you are discovering issues of sensitivity that were quite alien to you before. From a man's perspective it can be quite empowering, as women love a man who can communicate, especially about his feelings. I am also positive that this would be the same from all other perspectives. So it's important to not take advantage of your new-found wisdom, for you will only feel a sense of loss within if you abuse your new-found gift and you'll be back at square one each time. The choice is yours.

So you see, they are out there waiting to trick you back into a whirlpool of negativity. Being aware also makes you vulnerable at the beginning regarding other people but as you work harder and progress with your spiritual power, the more invisible you will become to the vampires of spirituality.

When you are learning to protect yourself from the vampires, it is not so much what you actually do to protect yourself but more about how you control yourself in environments that make you become a target to negativity and about how you maintain a level of positive awareness that supersedes others. You now know that the more aware you become the greater the number of negative people you will have to ignore, so the fact that you're aware of that gives you a headstart. If you know you're going to be in an environment that could damage the blissful day you have been having, it's important to arm yourself with some pretty powerful weapons: weapons of mental, positive power. This is where creative visualisation comes in handy.

We as humans have incredibly powerful conscious minds. We also have an entire, endless universe of knowledge within our subconscious, if we link the two together. As mentioned briefly before, we have an extremely powerful weapon. The journey that you have chosen, your spiritual journey, is all about positive mental ability put into action to create a positive mental change and outcome. What we think is who we are. What we are is how we have learnt. What we need to do is remember that if we have learnt in the right way, the positive way, we can create enough energy to project upon situations that can help to ease the way forward, hence creative visualisation.

Many people across the world have come to believe the power of creative visualisation. It has the ability to transfer energy into future situations. It's back to the same old, same old: belief. The more belief you have in yourself, the more power you can project.

Creative visualisation gives you a feeling of security. It allows you to walk into any situation you wish with a free and open mind ready for whatever is thrown at you. If, for example, you are going to a pub or nightclub and don't know who is going to be there, you need to project as much creative positive energy into that situation as possible. Not knowing who is going to be in your surroundings makes it that little bit harder. But practice makes perfect. The social environment is nearly always about a lot of trapped energies being thrown around uncontrollably by others. Many have had a hard day working. Some may have argued with loved ones. The point is that it is up to you to create a kind of positive force field around yourself before you get to the occasion.

Creative Visualisation Exercise

Sit in a quiet place within your own home, if possible. Some very soft music helps. Become as relaxed as possible until you feel a bit sleepy. Sitting or lying down is fine. Try if you can to clear away any thoughts that are flying in and out of your mind. If it is difficult for your mind to unwind, then focus on a lit candle if you have one, or on a colour in your mind. At all times keep yourself away from others. Start to concentrate on your breathing. Let your breathing become deep as you become more relaxed. After about ten or fifteen minutes, try to picture yourself in the pub. If you haven't been there it doesn't matter. Use your imagination. Focus in your mind on the fact that everyone is laughing and you're feeling really happy and content.

continued...

...continued

If any anxious feelings of insecurity pop in just listen to your breathing again until they go away. See yourself as the centre of attention, the person that everybody wants to talk to, and feel the positive energy they are projecting towards you. See yourself surrounded by a beautiful white light that gives you a sense of calm. See yourself having a fantastic night, without arguments of ill feeling from anyone. Continue to focus on this for as long as you feel is necessary. At the point you feel change, imagine that you're putting on your coat, or getting your things together to leave. Say your goodbyes to everyone and wish everyone a goodnight, with a big smile on your face. It is important that when you visualise this you feel a strong positive vibration oozing from within you onto the other people around you. Open your eyes – if they were closed – and sit, just for a minute or two. Then stand up and immediately go and do something else.

I have always found this to be a great way of giving myself a sense of security, a knowing that everything is going to be fine, and that the night is going to run smoothly, and fun will be had by all. You can easily transfer the same process to any situation –a meeting, an interview, even when traveling. If you are scared of traveling, picture the whole journey from start to finish as an easy and relaxed one. Creative visualisation is great in that it frees your worries from your conscious mind and stores the positive images within your subconscious. Treat yourself to a stress-free future, and give it a go.

3 The essential reasons for protection

WE HAVE TALKED VERY BRIEFLY in other parts of the book about protection, protecting yourself from any kind of negative energy, so let's now talk a little bit more in depth about the reasons for which we need to be fully protected.

As your journey takes you further away from the person you once were and a lot closer to the power within yourself, you need to be as protected as possible. We talked about the vampires of spirituality in the last section. This is just one area that needs to be in constant working order.

We also need be able to identify other ways in which negativity finds its way to us, but first we need to understand the reasons why.

To be spiritually ambitious is a challenge, a challenge for any human being. Anywhere in life that there are challenges, there are often dangers. The more you throw yourself into something like spirituality, the more you are in danger of becoming confused by who you are becoming, if you do not protect yourself. You can also end up bewildered and lost if you do not protect yourself. It is essential that you do not overlook protecting yourself and that it becomes part of your daily life. Some of you reading this may think that it is just one more thing that you need to think about, but have trust in these words: without protection you are completely on your own.

Protecting yourself is not only necessary on this journey that you have chosen but it also gives you exactly what you need. Protection is the ultimate sense of safety within the spiritual realm, which brings feelings of contentment. What people seem to forget is that when you are dealing with something as pure but powerful as spirituality, especially your own personal quest for spirituality, you are no longer dealing with the world as you know it. You are without doubt placing yourself in an incredibly vulnerable place, but as we have said: no pain, no gain. Learning to protect yourself in your daily life and understanding why you are doing it is good for everyone. If you're just reading this book because you are curious, and you don't feel ready to embark on your great spiritual quest, then I would advise you to still take note, as it can always come in handy, wherever you are in life.

At times in our lives we want to just go wild and run free into the future. But as with anything of a spiritual nature, you are creating and opening up such an incredible new world. Everything about who you are spiritually will eventually change. As you go through this growth period, you must stay aware of the dangers that await you. You cannot just push them aside without a care in the world. When something is so rich within its purity, it has to have ways in which to put you off. Just as much as we all want pure spiritual awareness, we have to earn it, and to earn it we have to fight for it. Therefore, we need our armour and our swords.

Try to imagine that spirituality is not just a feeling or a sense. Imagine it as a person living in the most beautiful place you have ever seen. Why would that person want just anyone coming to their sanctuary and spoiling it, spoiling it because they weren't ready to be there, because you didn't protect yourself correctly on your journey to the sanctuary? It is not that protecting yourself is good only for you, it is also good for others. You can't walk a true spiritual path without first making the road, and you can't make the road without the help of others. You will find that when you are practising the art of protecting yourself it involves protecting others around at the same time. Knowing this, you will find yourself becoming much more thoughtful towards others as they will become much more thoughtful towards you.

Creating a protective sense of energy around yourself and others is what will give you the drive to walk forwards on your spiritual quest, no matter how rough it may seem.

When you find yourself protecting yourself and others through a series of words that you will find further into the book, it will give you a sense of ultimate giving; a feeling of doing what is right. This is what gives you your power: protecting yourself and others.

Another key reason for protecting our spiritual energy is so that we don't misunderstand what our true goal is. As we open the doors of energy, they also close. The art of protection gives us the ability to open and close the doors ourselves, the doors being the energies passed from person to person. The energies are being transferred from different parts of time to allow a kind of linking formation to occur. The practice of protection allows us to soak up the positive energy and deflect the negative, thereby allowing us to follow the true path of spiritual energy to reach our destination. The less protected we are the more likely it is that we will walk through the wrong door on our way, and find ourselves going backwards rather than forwards. The more negative energy you encounter in your life through lack of protection, the more steps back you have to take until you have learnt to walk the path protected and pure. In doing that, staying protected, you will never misunderstand what your true goal is. Remember, give out the protective energy and focus on protecting yourself as this will give you much more positive power.

Another key reason, perhaps the most important reason, for spiritual protection is protection from evil. The word evil might sound a bit scary, like something from a horror movie, but it's best to be direct at this stage. It will keep you on your toes.

There are many different levels of spiritual awareness. You can be someone who progresses no further than finding a sense of well-being, all the way to someone who has found his or her path to become a spiritualist or medium. If you are fortunate enough to become somebody as gifted as that, you have to be very aware that you are dealing not only with small amounts of negative energy, but that you are tapping also into another world where good and evil are forever battling with each other. A medium or spiritualist is a person who channels to another time and gets their information from people who have passed over. If not fully protected when channelling, you could leave yourself at great risk of being spiritually attacked by a lost soul from the other side.

A lost soul is negative energy, or evil, as people working in the spiritual realm would call it. It is said that the lost souls are lost because they did something bad on the earth plane. I personally see lost souls as having lost their way through lack of direction. It's lack of protection that causes them to misunderstand their direction. In other words, it's as though they walked through the wrong door. If we keep our eyes and our hearts open while being protected, we will see things as a more spiritually aware person than otherwise we would not normally see. But if we walk alone without the support of our spiritual guides then we walk in fear of our purpose and our goal. Maintain the understanding that, regardless of what stage we are at on our spiritual journey, as long as we are protecting ourselves from negative energies, we will never walk alone. Our protection will guide us.

If at any time you feel vulnerable and feel as though you are losing your spiritual support, repeat in your mind the following words that have been written in the form of a prayer, a prayer of protection. It may appear to a lot of you that a prayer of protection seems a bit religious, but be assured that this book is written to start your ball rolling and to help you maintain a consistency with mental protection so that you are safer on your journey to spiritual awareness.

A PRAYER OF PROTECTION

Dear God
Please put the colour pink into my body for eternal love
Wrap us in crystals
Paint us silver
Paint us gold
Wrap us in mirrors
And place us in a pyramid
Filled with white light
So the white light goes through the apex of the pyramid
And wrap us in suits of shining armour
Please send out loving thoughts and prayers
To everyone we have met
Everyone we are meeting
And everyone we are going to meet.
God bless, Amen.

4 Trusting in your senses

ISN'T IT AMAZING? We are given all the clues, guided along a brightly-lit path, but yet we still let ourselves down by losing trust in our own senses. It doesn't matter what we are talking about, whether it be faith, turning knowledge into wisdom or learning to fight the vampires of spirituality, we must trust our senses, and trust what we feel. This is not about just our everyday senses, our outer senses. Yes, we need our outer senses to analyse the initial outcome for our conscious mind, but we also need our inner senses, our intuition. Knowing that no matter what happens our inner senses, or that deep, deep gut feeling, will never let us down, but learning to trust it completely… well, that's a whole different course of tests.

Picture the scene: you walk into a room filled with people on a night out. Do you a) look for any signs of negative energy so that you stay well clear and enjoy your night, or b) stroll on into the room without a care in the world accepting that whatever will happen, will happen? Some people say let it be. Whatever life throws at you, just let it happen. This is how you've probably been conducting your life, until now. Instead, try using that extra bit of time, spiritual sense, and brainpower to feel your way through the room. Trust in your senses to find the best place to sit. It's not as easy as it sounds. The place could be packed with people apart from two empty chairs at the bar. Your conscious mind says, "Hey, let's sit there as they are free." Your intuition, on the other hand, is jumping up and down saying, "No, no, no! Don't sit there. Something bad will happen. Don't sit there." It is at this point that you have to make a decision. Do you a) ignore your intuition and hope for the best, b) take your inner senses' advice and stand, or c) find another bar?

I have done this so many times, and often my friends think I'm a bit crazy. Well, they did at first but now if I say, "No, let's go somewhere else", they will go.

Example 1: Trusting your senses

I have always found that the best way to really learn to trust your senses is by making a point about how you feel to one person that is with you. If you are with just one person I suggest you try to persuade them to leave for some reason. If you are in a group, tell the person that you have doubts about staying where you are and that you would prefer to leave. Normally the other people with you will say, "No, let's stay here, it's OK." Famous last words! If your intuition has really been bugging you about it and you're trusting in your senses completely, make a note of the night. Try to remember if it went wrong. If anything seemed particularly bad or negative about the night, do not just put it down to coincidence. Say nothing more about it to your friends. Just make a mental note for yourself. The more this happens and the more you note the outcome, the more confident you will become in knowing that you are right. After some time, if you get that same feeling in your stomach, then you must do something about it. It does help if you tell the same person each time about your gut feeling. At least then they are also aware of what you are experiencing and they are more likely to stand by your side when you are trying to persuade your other friends that you feel something is not right.

Example 2: Trusting your senses

Another time that I often find my senses alerting me to a possible problem is when I'm about to walk into somewhere or about to walk down a road a certain way. If your intuition tells you, "No, you must not go that way, or go into that building," then do as it says. Stay clear of that direction. Start to listen to your self.

Sometimes you may be lucky enough to hear your own voice in your mind. Your inner voice may not be very loud to begin with. That has been known to happen a lot. Learning to listen will eventually become second nature and relative experiences will push you to listen and trust in your senses. You will see how becoming a purer more spiritually gifted person on the earth plane means big changes, changes for the better. Changes in these circumstances and listening to your intuition could save a lot of pain.

That may sound rather intense, but many lives might have been saved if the people in question had listened to their gut feeling before tragedy occurred. I feel it's very necessary for people everywhere to start becoming more aware of their own intuition. There are nasty people in this world. We can't change them but we can avoid them.

5 Seeing your power

LIKE A LOT THINGS IN LIFE, spiritual wisdom is very hard to find. It comes in all shapes and sizes and very rarely lets you see it unless you are ready. At this point in the book you need to understand where the journey may take you. If we, as human beings, try to force anything it never comes, correct? We need to relax and become graceful to truly see the power within us. We need to allow our souls freedom to roam the universe of spiritual knowledge to give us the opportunity to see the power we have within us. For some people, the simple idea of understanding the sentiment of peace and love can be very scary – or maybe even boring. By going back to the first half of the book, i.e. understanding the sense of what is written and appreciating its universal value, it will remind you that you can't earn your wisdom by cheating.

Seeing your power is about belief, forgiveness, love, and coping with loss. We are now entering into the part of the book which leaves no room for mistakes. If you have become the person so far that I hope you have from understanding steps one through to four, then you are ready to see your power. But if you have let the information go in one ear and out of the other, so to speak, we can go no further, as you might be disappointed with your own progress and results. Please be sure you are ready. Don't try to become something before you've become you.

The book itself is the process and journey you need to take to become spiritually aware. The end of the book will be the beginning for you, just the beginning of your journey through many spiritual encounters and spiritual moments that will leave you speechless.

You know when people talk about having a spiritual experience? Well, this could – and hopefully will – become something of a daily occurrence for you if you stick to your journey into spiritual development.

We all have the opportunity to see the power that has been given to us. What you must understand is that only some people find the path that uses certain levels of awareness.

When I talk about the power, I'm referring to the ability of being psychic or clairvoyant and/or clairaudient etc. First of all, we as human beings need to take the simple steps and become them, not to stray or deviate from the path of good. We all have the power within us. The power can be subtle and just give you a real sense of contentment or it can be extreme in that you become a kind of messenger with a very strong urge to give positive messages to others that can help. You don't know exactly why you feel the way you do, or why you have to give the information, or even how you know what you know. It just happens. The answers to questions about the ability to be super-spiritual and psychic is that not everyone can be that type of person if is not their destiny. The important thing to remember is to be happy with who you are, no matter what. Be grateful for small mercies.

Seeing your inner power is, quite frankly, amazing. It's like watching a video screen in your mind. You don't know how it's there, but it is. And very often than not, it's in colour. The best way to describe seeing your power is this: often in Hollywood movies there's a scene where someone is watching some old family super-eight home movies about a loved one who has passed away. The super-eight style home movie is how the power within you flickers in your subconscious mind first and then relays it to your conscious.

You really need to understand that you must not be too hard on yourself if you can't reach the higher points of spiritual success, as it may not be your destiny.

Seeing Your Power Exercise

Start to imagine a piece of information that relates to one of the first four steps. Focus on it. Close your eyes and keep your mind focused on the information. Let your mind wander, allowing space for visual images. Let yourself feel sleepy but stay awake. Allow yourself to start to go back to the actual time that relates to this feeling. Let your mind open itself up to you, drawing in on the energy from the past. As you do this, let your mind become visual to you. Try to see what is in the darkness behind your eyes. (One bit of advice: do not look for it; let it come.) As your image starts to appear, it may at first be broken up in flashes and hard to see. Just try to take anything from it that you can and write it down. Look for anything unusual in your image. If there is an image that you do not understand, don't worry. Often a friend or relative may have the answers. It is quite possible that you have forgotten certain points in your past. If not, make notes. Always remember, let the answers come to you. Do not force the issue of seeing your power. Let it arrive.

There is nothing wrong with learning from the past. Keep the faith. Know you will see your power and believe in your victory. If you stop now and decide not to put the groundwork in you will never know because you have to know the basics before you can be advanced.

6 Meditation – Part 1

ONE OF THE FIRST STEPS to creating the calm you need to fulfil your spiritual sanctuary is through meditation.

Meditation is one of the key factors to a greater spiritual existence. In part one we talk about the benefits of meditation and why we need to introduce this into finding spiritual success.

For hundreds of years, people all over the world have been training in many forms of meditation. The form of meditation you will learn in part one is for relaxation and protection. Meditation not only allows you to rid yourself of your daily stresses and worries but it also opens up an enormous doorway to another world, the world of spiritual knowledge, your home from home, the place that will probably become your only retreat from the pressures of daily life.

In earlier passages, we have very briefly mentioned small exercises that involved very basic forms of meditation. At this stage, we need to make concrete the most important areas of understanding a great state of meditation.

What we are talking about at this stage with meditation is the need to be able to relax and clear the mind from any day-to-day stresses or mental concerns. When you are at the beginning of such an immense journey into the spiritual world it is often very difficult to put down your day when you return home from a hard day's work, therefore many people find themselves stopping and starting to try to get their journey working for them. It can be very difficult if you are a single mother with three children or you have an elderly relative to look after. Maybe you feel you will never find the time for meditation. Just spare yourself one hour a day, preferably in the evening but anytime of the day would be OK. The great thing about a first step into meditation is that when you do find that hour, and work through a meditation, the calmness and sense of well-being that will be achieved afterwards will make you feel as though you can face any problem so much easier. So, as you can imagine, it is really worth trying to find that hour in which to start the ball rolling. For many of you, finding time may not really affect you, but it is important for everyone to have a chance at evolving his or her own spiritual success.

It is soon time for us to join forces and work through this meditation together. Before we do that, we need to consider how we are going to protect ourselves from any negative energy by use of our chakras.

Chakras are our main energy points located in different areas of our bodies. They create, when used correctly, an equal balance within our soul system. When used correctly, they allow us to become completely open to any energies that are wishing to enter into the conscious mind via the subconscious. If they are not used correctly it could prove to be disastrous to us in our personal lives.

The chakras in theory consist of seven points within the body. The eighth chakra will be explained later in the book. The points to learn and understand are as follows.

1 The base or seed chakra – situated at the base of the spine. It controls the instinctual side of us and governs our genetic makeup.
2 The pelvic chakra – situated at the genitals. It governs our energy and sex drive.
3 The solar-plexus chakra – situated at the navel. It governs our sense of personal power.
4 The heart chakra – situated over the heart. It governs our emotions.
5 The throat chakra – situated at the throat. It governs our ability to communicate.
6 The brow chakra – situated between the eyebrows. It governs our intellect.
7 The crown chakra – situated on the top of the head. It governs our spirituality.

It is vital that when you enter into any kind of meditation, be it just to relax or a full-blown meditation to reach higher planes, that you prepare yourself a) for a safe entry into a meditative state, and b) to create an equal and steady balance of energy to all the chakra points. They must be clear and ready to open.

Meditation Exercise I

First, sit comfortably. Second, close your eyes. Third, imagine that your chakra points are beautiful red roses that are closed tightly. Inside them are beautiful shining diamonds. On the outside of each rose, or each chakra point, there is a circle of white light. Imagine a rose. Starting with the base chakra, or seed chakra, you remove the circle of white light, you then see water fall upon the rose. The rose will then open to reveal the diamond. Take the diamond out of the rose and imagine a cloth cleaning the diamond until it's shining so bright it's nearly blinding. Then put the diamond back. Continue up the chakra points: the pelvic chakra, solar plexus chakra, heart chakra, throat chakra, brow chakra and crown chakra.

Once you have opened all of the chakra points and thoroughly cleaned the diamonds, imagine purple roots sprouting from the base of your feet going deep into the ground into the centre of the earth. This will keep you grounded while you are in your meditation. Now just continue sitting comfortably. Relax, and follow your breathing. Listen only to your breathing until it seems to take over your whole existence. Feel the peace starting to flow over your body. Remember, you are open but the roots going into the ground are keeping you safe. (A little tip: if you feel a little bit unbalanced or nervous, just simply imagine bright white light all around you; the brightest white light you have ever seen.) Continue to listen to your breathing. I recommend no more than fifteen to twenty minutes, but if you are really enjoying the feeling of pure relaxation, then do as you feel.

continued...

...continued

Once you have encountered your peace and tranquility, imagine a small pathway directly in front of you. At all times feel your breathing. See at the end of the pathway a door, a door glowing white with pure sunlight shining all around it. Slowly walk towards the door. You are safe, so don't worry. Walk up to the door feeling the warmth of the sunlight on your face. Reach for the door handle and open the door. At your own pace, walk though the door. As you walk through the door feel the warmth of hot sand on your feet. Hear the sound of waves beating against the shore. Feel the warm breeze blowing past you. See yourself on a beach. Let calm rush over you. There is no one else there, just you, sand dunes, the sea, the sun and the warm air. Walk down the beach slowly, feeling the sand between your toes; the sea air covering your face with such freshness and purity, you need to sit down. Sit and relax by the waters edge or lie down. Whatever you like. Just learn to use this beach as your place of freedom; your sanctuary. There is nobody there to harm you, nobody there to stress you out. Only peace and quiet exist. Stay relaxed on the beach for about twenty minutes. You may want to stay at the beach a little longer. Whatever you decide is OK. When you are ready to leave, stand up slowly and head towards the sand dunes at the top of the beach. As you walk towards them, you will see the doorway of white light once again. As before, open it slowly and walk back through, but this time feeling your feet on the floor of where you are sitting in your home. Feel your breathing becoming the focal point in your mind and stay calm, relaxed and peaceful for around five minutes. Then, as before, see your chakras, but this time starting with the crown chakra. See the diamond shining inside the rose. Imagine night falling upon the rose. Watch the rose close and then see the circle of white light surround the rose. Continue down your chakra points: brow chakra, throat chakra, heart chakra, solar plexus chakra, pelvic chakra and base or seed chakra. When you reach the base see your purple roots grow stronger around the floor of where you are sitting.

continued...

> *...continued*
>
> This will keep you grounded even when you have opened your eyes. When you do feel ready to open your eyes have the prayer of protection ready in front of you to read straight away.

Well, if you have followed that step by step you will have just completed your first Basic Meditation, Part I.

Now just sit, relax and think about what just happened and the way that you are feeling. It is always good to have a pen and paper ready to jot down anything you think or feel that has any importance to you, no matter how small. If you feel quite emotional when doing this basic meditation, do not worry. It is common for most people to feel emotional, because they have just entered their subconscious mind, maybe for the first time ever.

7 The dreams and nightmares

IMAGINE YOURSELF AS A SEED in the ground. This is what you were until you entered into your subconscious in the basic state of meditation. Now, you are a small green bud waiting to flower. By taking that chance and entering into your new world you have automatically opened up your subconscious abilities that little bit more.

When you are awake you have total control of your chakras. When you are in a state of deep sleep you do not. And because you have opened up your inner self your dreams will start to become much more vivid. You may also start having nightmares. This depends on whether or not you followed through on dealing with any of the issues in steps one to four. You needed to deal with your issues honestly because here is probably one of the first places that you decide to give up your journey. The nightmares may become too intense because you weren't honest with yourself. You may do all you can to stay away from meditation due to the fear of being too open. If you have messed up, then it's not too late to go back now.

The extremely positive side of this passage is that if you are ready to be at this stage then great!! You can learn so much from your dreams. I do like dream books for fun. Do you wake up remembering your dream, and run straight to the dream book too? But, that's just for fun. What you really need to do is try to analyse the image in your dreams. Write it all down. Write the dream down including your feelings.

Dreams are amazing. Sometimes they are straight to the point. Other times they are all about metaphor or symbolism. This is where you need to use that gut feeling we have talked about, your intuition.

Often, once you have started meditation and opening up your chakra points regularly, you will see a definite change in your personality, a change that is affected by your subconscious and conscious mind. This is why it is very important, once again, to be honest with yourself at all times. If you dream of a faceless person, or a person you don't recognise, doing something to you that makes you feel uncomfortable, and it just so happens that in your daily life you are feeling something similar to your dream, then you have to be honest and ask yourself what your dream is trying to tell you. Is it trying to warn you to end a relationship or confront the issue within the relationship that has been niggling you? Often dreams give you the greatest insight into your waking life. It's just about learning to believe what they say. People are always questioning their dreams, "I wonder what that dream was trying to tell me." Yet as they are saying it they probably already know. Their intuition is shouting at them from way inside. But the problem is that most people don't want to face their problems. If it is just a dream, what can it really mean? It's just a dream.

Do not be fooled into thinking that last statement could possibly be true. Why do you think scientists spend millions of dollars searching for the answers to dreams? For one reason, and one reason only – they know there is something to find. Let's face it, scientists, or any company or government for that matter, wouldn't go splashing out cash on something they thought wouldn't benefit them. Listen to your dreams; learn from your dreams. Grow from your dreams. You don't have to pay for them, and sometimes they can be real fun – so enjoy!

If you find that you are encountering a bombardment of nightmares ensure that you have closed down all your chakra points as talked about in Meditation Part I. Also, use the prayer of protection as often as you feel necessary. I use it throughout my whole day, especially before I sleep.

8 Staying grounded

A S WE HAVE BEEN TALKING about how magnificent it is on awakening to open your chakras and to find a new world, we also need to talk, before we move to the next chapter, about the consequences of forgetting the world we live in.

When life is hard and money is tight, and you have just split with your partner or you just can't take the daily pressures of life, you may forever find yourself wanting to go to the beach in your mind. This is not a good thing. I have been through this and feel it is very necessary to warn you. If you do feel this way and spend too much time in your self-meditation, forcing your subconscious for answers, you will end up going crazy. Not literally crazy, but more like mentally imbalanced. You can lose sight of what your goals are in life. You often drift apart from loved ones and lose friends that you have taken ages to find. This is why it is so important to stay grounded, to learn to balance the two worlds, and to divide your time equally.

Our lives are for living. The transitions from closed to open regarding our senses of awareness are merely a gift from the higher self. We must always respect our subconscious which is more powerful than us. Over time it will most likely teach us all we need to know about how to maintain that happy contented life that we are all searching for. Therefore, we must remember not to abuse our new-found wisdom but to show it respect by grounding ourselves as much as possible.

Staying grounded comes from the same kind of mindset as when you are meditating. When you wake up in the morning, after you have had your tea, juices or cereal, etc., give yourself five minutes to relax and concentrate.

You are probably saying, "The morning, I'll never have the time. I'm always late for work." Don't worry – this can be done in the shower or even on the toilet. It doesn't really matter, as long as you can visualise the images in your mind.

Staying Grounded Exercise

See yourself standing with loved ones you wish next to you. Stand in a room where you live that you feel most happy with. Now first say the prayer of protection. Then imagine beams of gold and white light coming from the ceiling of the room, down through the top of your head and down your body, where the white and gold light will pass down through your feet and back up into the room. Fill the room until you can't see anything but gold and white light. Ask for protection and support in your mind, for yourself and anyone with you. Imagine that it joins the gold and white light. At that point, imagine the light shooting back up through your body and through the ceiling of the room towards the sky.

After a short period of time you will be able to do this in a matter of minutes. There are a lot of people in the world that have many different rituals like this one. Many people may have up to ten rituals in one day. It's not something that takes up too much time once you have learnt the methods. The good thing about this exercise is it really does set you up spiritually – and mentally – for the day. You will leave your home feeling grounded, secure, safe and most of all protected.

Without having all the parts to the jigsaw of a spiritual journey, it could become very difficult to finish the puzzle. Stay grounded to enjoy your journey.

The unknown: exploring the mystical world

STEP SIX IS ABOUT MYSTICAL ENERGIES: who uses them, how they may be used, and how they affect daily life and the spiritual journey.

We now know how to build our foundation. We now know how to protect ourselves from unwanted negative energies, but what we need to know is how it can all be put to the test. Before we run through the practicalities, understanding the ideas, logic and wisdom behind today's psychics, mediums, clairvoyants, clairaudients and tarot readers would be a worthy journey within itself as some of you may very well end up being one of the above.

1 Psychics

PEOPLE HAVE BEEN BATTLING all over the world as to whether people can be psychic or not. Scientists are forever questioning the possibility that psychics are for real. Well, whatever they say, I have seen enough proof in my life to know that there are always going to be charlatans. However, when it comes to the real-deal psychic, watch out. They could possibly freak you out, but only in a good way.

A true psychic person works predominantly within the subconscious mind. The messages seen by a psychic person will often come to them in a quick succession of images. The images are often accompanied by very intense feelings that are thrown into the conscious mind. The mind itself is so powerful it is able to create a visual image, often right in the place of the crown chakra and brow chakra. The psychic person is often in a kind of semi-trance state when giving messages or information because the information comes so quick. It's as if you are grabbing at images in a split second and turning them into words, sentences, moments or even full situations that will happen in the future to the person you are reading.

'Reading' is the expression most commonly used to describe what psychics actually do when they are telling you the information that they see. They work with the information given with something called the unified field. This is the area of the subconscious only advanced spiritually aware people can tap into. Psychics have been around for many hundreds of years throughout the world. A psychic person does not look a certain way, speak a certain way or act a certain way. A genuine psychic person is often someone you would never expect to be psychic until they start telling you things about yourself that nobody else knows.

The purpose of reading this book may differ incredibly for different people. Some may like the idea of being able to help themselves to become better people whereas others may like the idea of becoming psychic themselves, by helping and giving to others. If you find yourself being thrown head first into the world of psychic vision, this is what you will have to do. When you are granted a gift such as being psychic, don't think for one minute it's only for your benefit, because it is not. The gift of being psychic is given to help those in need, to always put others first and to not complain. This is why I explained earlier that everyone has the ability to be truly spiritual, but to be psychic is not for everyone. As you are reading this now you must be honest with yourself and say to yourself, "Could I give up my life to help others?" When you are truly a visionary psychic, it does take over your path of life if you let it. And, if the day comes that you decide you need more time to yourself, it slides gently away. It won't disappear completely, it just moves a little further away than normal, and this makes it harder for you to grab at the visual messages. But before any of this is possible, from the beginning you must be sure you want to help others.

You need to know what you would be letting yourself in for if you were to take on the role of a psychic. If being a true psychic is not for you, you still have the opportunity to reach a higher level of awareness, where you can interact with your guides. This will be covered later in the book.

Psychics really do exist and they are an amazing power within life. They can help you by offering you information you would not otherwise be aware of, but only if you believe. "Why should the guide dog guide the blind person without the blind person first believing in the dog?" If you don't believe in what the psychic person is telling you even when there is unquestionable proof in what they are saying, why should you be given the opportunity to have the insight into true untainted wisdom for your benefit? I have come across so many people who just want to take the wisdom from the psychic and run. But to make matters even more frustrating is that they seem to take only what they want from the information given. This is not a good thing. When you have a reading from someone psychic you must deal with all the information given or not deal at all. It is your choice. Be warned: if you don't take all the information given, you may find yourself worse off.

People who have readings have to understand that if they are told something they don't want to hear because it is part of an issue that they haven't dealt with, things get worse. They must not blame the reader. There are too many people in denial. Yes, that is their choice, but why ask a psychic person for help if one is in denial? That doesn't help anyone, the reader or the person who has the reading. It is important to add this part to let anyone out there thinking about having readings know what is involved and what they are truly going to get when the reader is a true psychic.

There are, of course, the fakes who give the true psychic a bad name. It is always best to get a recommendation for a great reader. Stay clear of psychic chat lines or people who give out flyers on streets. The true psychic will always have a queue of people waiting to see them because of the true nature of their ability. They don't have to sell themselves. Their wisdom sells itself.

What I do understand, and what I have learnt about the human race on my own quest for higher knowledge, is that the human race is full of fear. As soon as they are unsure about something because they can't control it or they don't understand it, they dismiss it. Frankly, I find this quite amusing. Face the fear, overcome it and join the rest of us on the quest for brighter things in life, where people walk the earth with an open mind.

2a Mediums/spiritualists

MEDIUMS ARE QUITE DIFFERENT in the way that they read. A medium is a type of spiritualist who has a direct link to the 'afterlife', sometimes called spirit world.

When we talk about the spirit world, we are talking about the place in which the deceased reside. The spirit world is where spiritualists and mediums get all their information to give to others. I have always seen mediums as very warm, caring people who are extremely in touch with life itself.

Mediums often receive information from people they knew or from people their client knew who passed away, such as grandparents, parents, friends, American Indians or even monks. Depending on what information needs to be given will determine the guide.

The most amazing and fascinating thing I have personally experienced with mediums is their ability to see accurate details of people who have passed. It has always amazed me.

Some people I know will never believe. They could be talking to a medium who tells them they have their grandmother with them. The medium may tell them that their grandmother had only one eye, which was false and yellow and that her hair was blue with pink spots. "Yes, that's right, she did," the person would say, "but that's just a coincidence." You see some people are not meant to believe, but that is their destiny. As long as you do, or you at least try to keep an open mind when dealing with mystical issues, that is all that counts.

Some of you will have already had many readings from mediums. Some of you may be readers yourselves. Some of you may be hoping and wishing that you to will be able to develop a level of ability within the psychic realm by the time you have finished this book. Whatever the outcome, just enjoy your journey, whether you become a medium or not.

If you feel that you need to find a good reader to help you on your journey it is often good to find your nearest spiritualist church. Go there one evening and you will be given information by the right medium, if there is some information to be given. The medium may very well be channeling directly from a relative of yours or a loved one in the spirit world. If the medium gives you a message, take the message with an open heart and mind. It is important that there is good proof that only you would know, or that relates to you, personally. I must admit I have seen some mediums that were not as accurate as others, which is why it is important to be either recommended in the first instance or to have the proof. Another point I wish to add on behalf of mediums is that if anyone wants to visit a medium at any time, always allow the medium time to get into the reading to see the visions and the words to give. You must remember that to many a medium you are a stranger. A good medium will often be able to accurately see your whole life, past, present and future in only a half-hour or an hour session. That is amazing. To be sure you are aware, make sure your reader does not probe you for answers. If they do, it is likely they are fake.

On a much more sensitive note, when you do find the right medium for you, you might find the sessions very emotional, even sometimes quite upsetting. I know how very difficult it can be to cope with losing a loved one. And when you know your loved one is in the room with you and the medium, it can be overwhelming. There is, of course, an incredible sense of love and supernatural power at the same time, which may make you fearful. Stay calm. You know what is happening in the room. You feel it but you can't explain it. My advice is to just go with it.

Let go of any preconceived ideas that you previously had about seeing the medium, and just let it happen. One of the most beautiful experiences anyone could have is knowing that their loved one is with them and knowing that they will see them again, that this is not the end. This may, in fact, be just the beginning.

There is a major point that has to be made regarding having readings. This point is that when readers are very talented they can make you feel that it is important to run your own life, without first consulting them. This is understandable as they can be truly amazing when they give you information so accurate that you feel lost without them. This is not a habit you need to develop. Personally, I believe you should have a maximum of two readings a year. You'll need to give the information time to unfold in your relative life. Many people across the world have found themselves becoming hooked on spiritual readings. This is what you must take from readings: guidance. You can then use the wisdom given to you to have a clearer picture of your own existence and future. Be wise; don't be greedy.

2b The trans-medium

THE TRANS-MEDIUM is something very different indeed and a form of reading that you need to be very aware of. There are very few trans-mediums in the world. Firstly, it is because it is a gift that needs an incredible amount of focus and spiritual ability. Secondly, it has been known to be dangerous to the reader.

The trans-medium acts as a direct energy link to the spirit world. Unlike the normal medium, the trans-medium acts as a kind of host for a spirit to enter. As you can imagine some of the consequences can be severe, such as possession, death and mental illness.

There have only been a few recorded and logged accounts of true sessions that have taken place with trans-mediums. This kind of reading is not the type of reading I would advise anyone who is reading this book to go to, even if you did find a trans-medium that was the genuine article.

3 Clairvoyants/clairaudients

MOVING ON TO THE NEXT FORM OF READING is a mix between the psychics and the medium/spiritualists.

First of all we have the clairvoyants. A clairvoyant is sometimes pictured as a little old lady with a crystal ball, sitting in a small window at the front of her seaside house, wearing a tacky headscarf. Sadly, this picture of the clairvoyant is old-fashioned. I have come across a whole new level of clairvoyant readers over the past ten years that have made a mark in the world of spiritual practice. The genuine clairvoyant is a spiritual visionary that would stand up to any proof test.

The clairvoyant sees, but does not hear, messages. The messages come to the clairvoyant via the video-type image found at the brow chakra. It is much like the psychic image but more in-depth. The image is seen more like a mini movie. It's doesn't flicker like the psychic images.

The point about the clairvoyant is that the information given will be the information that was supposed to be given. The clairvoyant does not channel from the spirit world or speak to spirits, which might make some people feel more comfortable when having a reading.

Bear in mind that a clairvoyant can very rarely see the past, unlike the medium/spiritualist. Normally they can only see the future. It's wise when finding out information on different types of readers not to overlook clairvoyance because it has a definite sense about the future, as that is its primary goal. It is advisable to try a few different readers in your lifetime as it is not always easy to know who should read for you if you yourself have no psychic ability. If you really feel ready to try to get through to a loved one, then have a reading from a medium/spiritualist. If you want to know about the future, see a clairvoyant or someone who is clairaudient.

A clairaudient is someone who does not see any type of visual imagery at all. They only hear messages. The messages, once again, are only for the person that they are reading. Clairaudients are often associated with readers that are in their early stages of spiritual development. To anyone reading this who hasn't experienced any type of psychic message, the feeling you get when receiving an audio message is amazing.

In speaking to many different readers I found that nearly all had a common feeling that the clairaudient was often what came first if they were readers with an all-round ability. You see, many readers can be all we have talked about and sometimes a little bit more. Sometimes people have been known to work within the eighth chakra. We will talk about that a bit later on.

4 Tarot (the tarot cards)

THE **TAROT CARDS** are becoming one of the most widely used forms of spiritual merchandise the world can offer. In many shapes, designs and meanings, the tarot cards have enabled anyone to buy a deck at any gift shop, read the guide book and then have fun playing spiritual guru. I may say that in jest, but for many people that's all it is – a bit of fun. For others, it is taken very seriously. People make a lot of money from reading tarot cards. It helps the person who is having the reading because they can see something in front of them, and it also helps them to believe.

The exciting thing about tarot is that when you research it you will find that it goes back many, many years and over centuries it grew to have magical powers. This is only possible if the person reading the tarot had psychic abilities in the first place. You see, the magic is not in the cards; it is in the person reading them. If you go to a tarot card reader who has no psychic ability whatsoever, you might as well buy a pack yourself. On the other hand, if a tarot reader was recommended to you by a friend who was amazed with their reading, then go. I have always felt that it is a bit like 'pot luck' when going for tarot card readings, but there is no harm in trying.

5 The eighth chakra

NOW WE WILL TALK about the most powerful point of awareness. The eighth chakra is a vision for many, but reality for few. The eighth chakra sits above the crown chakra and is the all-knowing, heavenly chakra. It acts like an open channel directly to the spirit world, enabling the reader to gain infinite wisdom and knowledge. The eighth chakra is very rarely talked about, as many people who have not yet encountered it do not believe that it exists. It does exist, but only to each individual reader who is ready to embrace its power.

The eighth chakra is the purest form of sacred ability and wisdom, at this point, that is known to anyone within the spiritual network. It is different in that the energy field that it creates is so much larger than any of the other chakra points. Its width is the size of the top of the head and runs upwards like a jet stream into the heavens. People who have experienced the eighth chakra will understand that it is the final piece of the spiritual internal jigsaw. It gives the reader a sense of infinite knowledge that seems to come from somewhere long ago. It gives pure spiritual belief and universal understanding. You may never experience your eighth chakra, but if you do, be prepared for your mission and journey on this planet as you will be forever changed. But don't worry; if you do experience it, you will know when, how and why you have. Recognise only that you would be a type of messenger for God.

The eighth chakra talks of visions of the future. It talks of great fires sweeping through two of the largest cities in the world in 2013. It talks of a great government infrastructure being created, a type of giant government that will rule the world. It talks of how planes will be able to fly faster than the speed of light. Who knows what the future holds, but I see the world in quite a desperate state spiritually, so I feel we must do all we can to be solid and strong, and individual within ourselves. Then, and only then, can we join together to create a greater spiritual alliance.

The eighth charka, in my eyes, is the purest most spiritual weapon of the future. People who are able to use their eighth chakra will be the leaders of the new spiritual world, the leaders who will join forces to fight against the darker energies that exist on the planet. The eighth chakra also talks of three separate governments, two English-speaking governments and one foreign, all plotting to deceive the rest of the world through the media with plans to make the world's economy a greater one for the people. That, of course, will be a lie to benefit the governments in question financially. Why is it that we need to listen to anyone else at all regarding the future of ourselves and of our children? Be aware of a powerful man giving flowers to the nation and be ready to stand up against evil.

This is all information given to me by someone with the power of the eighth chakra. As far as I can see the chakra itself is the ultimate tool of vision. It seems to be just as important as all the other chakra points put together.

This section may have seemed a little bit 'out there', but it is something that needed to be mentioned for you to be aware of.

6 Spiritual healing

WE ARE ALL HEALING in our everyday lives. Even the smallest gesture is healing. A kiss to a loved one, helping an old lady to cross the road, or paying that little bit of extra attention to your child. We are all healing in our own ways every day, without even knowing it.

Healing is, to me, a sense of the purest life force. It is without doubt one of the most practised alternative therapies on the planet. You can go pretty much anywhere in the world, find an alternative therapy centre and get some kind of healing treatment.

Healing as a treatment can help many sick people and has gained respect from the average man or woman to kings, queens, presidents and prime ministers.

There are many forms of healing. One of the most commonly used is when the healer holds his or her hands about an inch or two off the body enabling a flow of healing energy to pass through the healer to the client. The more advanced healers will be using both hands whereas many of those people who have just been granted the use of their gift just use one hand.

The difference between other forms of spiritual practice and healing is that the energy flow is different. The psychic will use a flow of energy that runs back and forth between the client, whereas the healer will act as a kind of conductor of healing energy. The energy will pass through the healer from the head down through the body, and then through the palms of the hands and out of the fingertips. Instead of going around the body of the healer, the energy shoots straight down in a continuous stream, like a bolt of lightening.

Having healing done on any part of your body is highly recommended. I have had healing many times, and have always found the results to be good. The one thing I do find about healing is that it doesn't last forever. I did go back to one healer several times for the same medical problem. It was a problem in my lower back. The healing felt great and the result lasted for anything from three weeks to six months. When I was having the healing I could actually feel the changes that were occurring within my body. For me, that is a miracle. There could very well be healers in the world, perhaps in the invisible tribe of the Amazon, that could heal me forever but I haven't yet discovered them.

Healing is definitely a form of spiritual work that is more socially acceptable compared to psychics and mediums. So, if you decide that healing is something you feel you have in you do not be afraid to talk to someone about it.

Lots of healers find out that they have an ability to heal purely by chance. They might be helping a friend or loved one and find out that somehow they took away a headache or backache by putting their hands on the person in question. This is quite often the way healers start their journey in the world of healing. Try the following exercise to find out whether or not you have been given the gift of healing.

Healer Exercise

Sit with a friend in a quiet place in your home. Ask your friend to sit or lie down, depending on where their pain is. Open your chakras and focus on getting the answer to where the real problem stems from within your friend. Often the area where there is pain is not the source of the problem. So let your subconscious mind bring the answer to you. Let your hand or hands be guided to the spot. If you feel only one of your hands drawn to the area, that's fine. Do not force the other. Quite often it is the right hand that people have found to be a more powerful conductor for healing energy. Once your hand is over the area you feel is the source of the problem, hold your hand or hands over the area about two inches from the skin or clothing. The test as to whether or not you are a healer is if the palm of your hand starts to become very hot, even sweaty, and your friend can also feel the heat. If this starts to occur imagine a beautiful flow of white light shooting down through the top of your head, down through your body and into your friend, allowing the flow of energy to pass through your body until you feel the job is done.

Do not heal for more than an hour, but do give the energy time to do its magic. If you find that you are walking into the world of healing others congratulate yourself on your healing journey. If you have not tried any type of healing but wish to, try reiki healing. Reiki is a great way to start understanding the benefits of spiritual practice.

7 Past lives

PEOPLE HAVE MANY DIFFERENT IDEAS about where we come from and whether or not this is the only life we have lived. Let us consider the belief that we have had many other lives and whether or not it could be true.

Are we living just one life, or have we lived two, three or maybe even hundreds? Some people say they see their other lives in their dreams. Others say we are brought back to a new life, time and time again, until we have learnt the lessons that are dealt to us.

This is what I believe: if we did have many lives, it would be because we need to learn more and more about our souls and how they can help us and others. I do believe that for many people there may never be an ending to their learning in this life, so it is highly likely that they may have to return once again to another life to try once again to pass the tests that are given to them.

People often question that if we don't go to an after-life we must be bad people and go to hell. Well, that is one place I don't quite believe in.

I like to think that it is more like a transitional movement that we are dealing with on that subject, one place to another, one life to another. It is one of those topics that can be discussed for hours and hours at a party. It is a decision that only you can make yourself. But there is one way to find out whether or not you have lived other lives, and that is past-life regression.

Past-life regression is a very deep form of meditation. Basically, a past-life regression practitioner has the ability to take you back to your past lives. It's similar to hypnosis, but with a twist. It can be a very serious subject, and one that needs to be taken with tentative steps. If you open the door to a spiritual world you have to be sure that you are able to deal with what you find. If you decide to have past-life regression, then make sure you close your chakras after the session and say the prayer of protection as often as you feel you need. I have met many people who have had past-life regression and they all seem to have a similar reaction: shock. They are shocked because they can remember their past lives and how situations, people and events taking place in this life often feel like they are a reflection of another life. This is why it is important to be careful what you wish for, and to never judge or mock something you know nothing about, for you might just be making a mistake that cannot be undone until your next life.

8 Deja vu

EVERY SINGLE ONE OF YOU will have had some sort of deja vu experience in your lifetime. I have personally had countless episodes of deja vu. Some lasted for up to a minute in length. Deja vu has baffled scientists for years. It is an episode of brief awareness of a time or moment that you recognise as extremely familiar to you, even if you do not recognise your surroundings in your present state of mind. Deja vu can also become apparent at any point, whether you're at home, at work, or just driving along. I often have deja vu at home, where I feel something good is about to happen. For everyone the reaction is different, so people may have a different sense of what deja vu brings to their life. For me it is only good luck, often in the form of financial rewards.

This brings us to the point where we need to ask the question, "Does deja vu have any relation to past lives?" For people who are experiencing deja vu in an unfamiliar place it is likely the feeling is, "I have been here before. I know this place." Could this mean that you have been there before in a past life? That you are reliving an experience whereby you needed to learn a lesson that you previously failed? It is something that people have always discussed. Personally, I feel that any type of deja vu that leaves you feeling that you have been there before is most probably a moment in time where time has stopped and shown you the past life. I also believe that if that is the case, then you most probably lived in that past life not too long ago. It is an extremely bizarre phenomenon, and I am sure it will have people guessing for centuries to come.

Speaking to God: Taking your journey a step further

7

1 The art of channelling – Meditation Part II

IT IS NOW TIME FOR US to try to put some of our learning and understanding to the test. We have talked very briefly about a few different elements of spiritual practice: mediums, psychics, healers, etc. You have also understood the first four steps. Now it is time to try to bring the two together to help you understand the advantages of being able to put yourself into a state of mind through meditation to channel to the other side, to channel to the spirit world and, if possible, to receive a message from one of your guides.

The art of channelling is an incredibly serious part of your spiritual practice that has come from great ancient leaders of spiritual understanding, such as American Indians and monks. It is your first step to really appreciating how to become the new you.

The above sections that discuss spiritual practices will give you an idea of what is possible were you to become a channeller, a spiritualist or a medium.

Let's now focus on a breathing exercise. The breathing is exceptionally important in this exercise, as it will keep you balanced as you start to channel.

Breathing Exercise

Find a quiet place to sit for about two to three minutes, just to get yourself completely relaxed. Try to sit upright with your back straight and your feet flat on the floor, so that the alignment of your body is correct. Now close your eyes and start to concentrate on your breathing. Breathe slowly and deeply putting your hands on your stomach. Try to breathe deep into your diaphragm. Feel your stomach moving in and out as you breathe. Keep up the breathing for about five to six minutes, feeling the oxygen circulating in your body. Now, try to feel the oxygen in all the areas of your body. Start at your toes. As you breathe in feel the air going down into your toes. Now, go up your body from your ankles, to your legs, to your knees, waist, stomach, chest, throat and finally into your head. Feel the oxygen powering around your relaxed body, allowing your body to feel relaxed but powerful with all the air that it is being given.

Now open your chakras in the same way as in Meditation Part I, using the rose with a clean diamond. Open the chakra points starting from the base chakra working up to the crown chakra. Then visualise the colour purple all around your body. This will give you spiritual clarity and strength. Imagine the roots coming from your feet into the ground, remembering to stay seated at all times with your eyes closed.

Where we go from here now is slightly different to Meditation Part I. (By separating the meditation, you won't become confused with what you are trying to achieve.)

Meditation Exercise II part 1

Imagine yourself in a room. The room is all white and there is just one doorway, one table and a chair. Imagine that you are wearing very soft and comfortable white linen robes. Sit at the table. In front of you, there is a sheet of paper and a pen. Look at the paper. Write down on the paper the name of a loved one who has passed away who you would love to see again. Write down the name eight times and then close your eyes while you are in the room. Do not get up off the chair and walk around. Just sit and relax, listening to your breathing until you feel a need to leave the room. It shouldn't be more than fifteen minutes. Now, look down at the paper and see if anything else has been written on the paper, if so great. If nothing further has been written, then don't worry.

To move on to the next part of the meditation does not need an answer on the paper, but often there is some kind of message. Some people think the messages come from their own mind. Some believe the message has come directly from the person who is now in the spirit world. Make your choice as to what you believe, but be sure to make the right choice to get the most out of this channelling meditation.

Meditation Exercise II part 2

Whether there was a message on the paper or not, remain sitting on the chair and look down on the floor to the left of you. You should see a golden key. Pick up the key and walk towards the door. Put the key in the door and turn it. Open the door. As you are opening the door you will be overcome by a very bright white, nearly blinding light. Walk through the light and into a small charming garden, with beautiful flowers all around the edges and two great big oak trees. Just underneath the oak trees to your right, you will see a bench. Walk over to the bench and take a seat.

continued...

...continued

Look around at just how beautiful the garden is, smell the flowers. Check if you notice any small birds flying around, and try to make a mental note of them and anything else you see. If you look down to your left leg you will see you have a pocket. Reach into the pocket and pull out an envelope. Your name should be written on the front. Open it. Inside there may be a time written for you to come back to the garden to get a message or speak face-to-face with your loved one from the spirit world. If there is no time do not worry. It just means that it is not your time, to see what you want to see. You will need to keep coming back to the garden until the time is right.

If you feel you are getting a bum deal, remember that it is more important that you are ready, for your sake. The spirits do not want to hurt or upset you. They need you to be strong and clear of any issues. If you don't receive any messages at this point, know that you are probably not being totally honest with yourself about your progression.

Meditation Exercise II part 3

Last of all, get up from the bench. Look for the large gate at the end of the garden. Walk towards the gate. Walk straight through by opening the gate. Walk through the white light and feel yourself fall back into your body. You should feel very heavy in your body, but that's fine. Just remain seated with your eyes closed until you start to feel yourself again. Now start closing your chakras starting with the crown chakra all the way down to the base chakra.

You have once again completed closing down.

I hope you were able to find a message at this point, but if you didn't, please don't worry. It can take quite a time to develop your belief system in a channelling meditation. One last thing: it might help if you have a friend to come to help you by talking you through the meditation so that you can keep your eyes shut. Together you can sit amongst candles and soft music. If you can't find anyone suitable, once again, don't worry. See it as an opportunity to create for yourself a beautiful experience.

What you have just seen is channelling in its simplest form in meditation. This is your very first step into hopefully making some kind of contact with your guides. The art of channelling is a spiritual practice, widely used by spiritual gurus and leaders. Generally, they do not need to spend such a great deal of time in meditation because their experience and abilities are already quite incredible. They often channel for hours, channelling very long messages, visions or even maybe whole books or scriptures. Do not concern yourself with becoming a spiritual leader at this point. Just take small steps in your journey into channelling.

A small tip

Always remember to keep your mind free of any day-to-day thoughts when you are in the meditation. This will help you to differentiate between true messages from a true guide while on the bench in the garden and a message that appears from your conscious mind. Make a note of any changes in your meditation no matter how small, not forgetting to record all messages you receive.

Good luck.

2 Receiving a message

FOR MANY OF YOU reading the text so far, it may be a slightly different journey from what you had expected. You need to understand what becoming spiritually aware really means. We could talk for days about the laws of spirituality but, to be honest, it wouldn't take you to the place in which you wish to go.

Some of you may feel a bit apprehensive as you get to a stage in meditation where you start to receive messages from your spiritual guides. I hope to bring the basic understanding behind the real meaning of the word 'spiritual'.

Western society often frowns upon different ideas of spiritual practice. Look at the Tibetan monks and the American Indians and you will not only be looking at an amazing race of people, but you will also be looking at the ultimate channellers. People either seem to misread what Tibetan monks do within the meditative state or they find it difficult to relate to their methods which are in fact very similar to ours. They receive messages just as we can.

What is the point in going through life being afraid of something so amazing? Do not be afraid of receiving a message. Firstly, if you are afraid and want to receive a message, it probably won't come. Secondly if you are afraid full stop, don't worry. You might just find that what was once not for you, is about to become your ideal source of inspiration and information.

As explained in Meditation Part II, you can create a direct link with your spiritual guides. Ask for messages to help you along your way in life. Some of you may find that you're meditating for long periods before receiving any sort of message. As I have said, it just might not be your time for receiving messages, as it does take one hundred per cent belief. For others, the messages may be coming through thick and fast. If you just happen to be extremely spiritually aware but didn't know it, you might find it overwhelming at first if you sense a lot of messages trying to come to you. Whatever your experience may be, always remember to open and close your chakras correctly at all times.

If you feel a little scared when you go into meditation, then don't do it for a short period. You may find that messages or snippets of messages that you receive are things you are being made aware of in your daily life. My advice to you if you have received a message, particularly if it is your first, is to be happy. No don't be happy, be amazed. If you open the envelope while in your meditation with a truly clear mind and controlled breathing and there is something written on the paper inside, then wow! You have started the main part of your true journey into becoming spiritual.

Try to imagine in your mind what it really means to receive a message from a spirit guide from another dimension. It sets you apart from so many other people. The really great thing about it is that when you do receive the message or messages they will more than likely prove themselves, as long as you keep your mind open. The messages will relate to something significant in your life, something that makes you feel, frankly, quite freaked out. This is because the reality of the message will finally sink in that this does exist. It is real. You have connected with an unfamiliar life force.

The reality of receiving a message is that you can start to run your life in a completely different way. You will start to find you have the ability to determine certain things in your life. You will be able to hold within you an extra set of eyes and ears that allow you to see decisions you would normally make, but in a brand new light. The reality of receiving messages helps you achieve a much higher standard of living because you are able to think more clearly, and more accurately about future decisions. Remember, at first you will most likely just receive a small number of messages, possibly even just one. When you decide to kick your non-belief to the kerb and make headway into an unknown destination, it's likely that you will take things slowly. So, don't worry if at first you only receive a short message, or even the same message over and over again.

As you can imagine, the likelihood that you are already honed within your conscious mind to understand everything that is changing due to meditation is doubtful. Therefore, you may also find it difficult to decipher the message or messages that you receive. You will quite often come to learn that things are not always as they seem. I believe that your guides like to put you to the test to see if you're genuine in your pursuits. They need to see if you have what it takes; ultimately, to learn the meanings behind your messages and to use them wisely to change whatever needs to be changed in your life.

However you do decide to deal with any kind of message you receive is entirely up to you. You can choose to dismiss it and continue with your life as you did before, or you can be brave and honour your journey and your guides for blessing you with the gift of insight. I have always found meditation to be such a great way to help me find my way into working with my guides. It always makes me feel secure to know that if I don't let them down, they won't let me down.

Once again, if you haven't yet received a message, continue trying. Do not give up on yourself.

3 Working with your guides

Note: When entering into any spiritual practice always remember to open and close your chakras.

AFTER RECEIVING A MESSAGE it is very important to try to understand how to work with your guides and how to maintain a constant and consistent energy line between yourself and your guide in question.

The way in which you do this simple exercise is as follows.

> ## Meditation in Discovering your Guide
>
> Firstly, sit quietly and clear your mind. Start by working on your breathing exercise until you start to feel very relaxed. Try to visualise the guide in question who is sending you the message. It may not be a family member or the person you asked for in Meditation Part II. It may be another guide that is there for you for a certain purpose. You have to appreciate that sometimes it may be difficult to make the connection with family members or loved ones who have passed for many reasons, one being they are too afraid to approach.
>
> When you feel very relaxed and you have started to try to visualise your guide, let your mind just wander. Think of nothing. Listen to your breathing. Look into the darkness behind your eyes. Quite often the face of the guide in question will slowly start to appear in your mind. Do not be afraid or allow your conscious mind to dismiss the image that appears before you. Allow yourself to believe what you see. Often, the image at first will be unclear. This is because the guide will often only show you certain parts of themselves. It is like a blurred picture that at points becomes clear. If you are fortunate enough to experience this, then hold it close to your heart and do not talk to many people about it.
>
> *...continued*

...continued

That would create too much negativity around your progress. Whether you see a vision of your guide's face or not, follow the instructions to the next stage.

Remain where you are and continue your breathing pattern. Now, try to visualise in your mind something that inspires within you thoughts of happiness and love. When you are feeling happiness and love in your mind, heart and body, send a small token of your appreciation out to your spiritual guide, regardless of whether or not you know them. Imagine your feelings in the shape of a ball, a golden ball. Be thankful for your life and your ability to love and send this thought spinning around the ball. Now, imagine the ball flying into the darkness.

This meditation allows you to maintain an understanding with your higher self and your guides, to show them that you are worthy and that you are not trying to achieve greater abilities within a spiritual practice for self-gain. The moment you decide to take, to use or abuse the gift of wisdom and knowledge, your guides will stop giving you messages. You will then feel a kind of internal loneliness, as though a door has been closed on you. This is for a good reason, for the moment that you decide to work against the wishes of your true destiny, you become a danger to yourself and to others. I have known some people who have gone off the rails and started believing that they were some kind of super human, or even a god. The truth is that we are all able to channel and to work with guides.

Now that you have understood the need for respect and friendship to be built, let's can carry on.

There are many benefits to working with your guides. For example, it allows you to throw a thought out into the universe through your subconscious at any time and wait to see the answers when you go into your next meditation. It also allows your higher self to build your new pathway for you to become so much bigger and brighter. When the moment comes that you decide to believe one hundred per cent in what is truly happening to you, your guides know you are ready. Again, you must believe in yourself, in your guides and in your journey or you will get nothing. You will see only a blank page in meditation or within spiritual practices. It's obvious really. Why would you believe in someone who doesn't believe in you? Work with your guides to brighten your future for yourself and your loved ones.

It is also said that once you have started to build the foundation of a relationship with your guides, they will start to help you in your everyday life, without the need for meditation. You won't receive messages as clearly as in meditation at this early stage. However, they will plant thoughts in your mind to make you see things in your conscious mind very differently.

You may be just strolling down the street and sense something is wrong. You may be just about to cross the road, and a car shoots out of nowhere. Normally you would just dismiss it for that spilt second and continue to walk across after the car has gone. But as you have now started to walk this new spiritual path you will feel very differently about the incident. You will realise that the more you are in touch with your guides, the more aware you become. Belief is always the answer. Believe in the messages that are sent to you. As you start to notice what's happening in your life, the higher your awareness becomes until it is second nature to listen to your higher self.

4a Embracing their wisdom

AS YOU SLOWLY BUT SURELY PROGRESS through your meditations, you will start to see a pattern emerging. It will be a series of feelings for those who haven't yet received a message. You will start to see a picture being built, a picture of the beginning of your spiritual journey. As you will appreciate, you have been living predominantly within your conscious mind until you entered into your journey. Therefore, you are still at your very early stages within the understanding of your purpose. This is why more proof will be shown to you to help you deal with whatever needs to be dealt with in your everyday life.

To embrace your own spiritual guide's wisdom, you must have that very special trust. To walk a path blind is the easiest thing to do, but as long as you remember you are no longer blind when you have the faith, the path will become very clear. Just trust in what your purpose is for this journey you are taking.

Believe me when I say I know how it can feel starting this wild new spiritual journey. One minute you are living this perfectly normal, unclear, faithless, simple life and the next you are supposed to believe in guides. I started my journey with an open mind, but also a little bit skeptically. But as the proof unfolded before my eyes, my belief became stronger. I will never look back.

What can you possibly lose by putting out your arms and embracing beauty, wisdom and freedom? How could that be a bad thing? Don't let yourself be judged by others. Keep your discovery of yourself to yourself. Help others quietly. As soon as you start to have the one hundred per cent trust in yourself, you will start to feel as though there is not one thing that you cannot overcome. Sadness seems positive. Loneliness becomes a time to reflect. Anger becomes an alien. All the very present issues in your daily life start to become non-existent. The more you listen the more you grow. The more you grow, the wiser you become. It can be an awakening of such beautiful measure that I am sure you will never look back.

It is also important to remember that you must be totally sure of your ability; that when you embrace the messages given, you are aware of the whole message. You must also be aware that once you've started this journey, you must keep on top of your spiritual self. Life could become difficult if one day you receive messages, and the next you don't. Be sure that you are honest in where you are at on your journey at all times. At this point, people often think they are ready to start sorting out other peoples' lives before they have sorted out their own. Big mistake. Never, never feel you are ready to help others until you are one hundred and fifty per cent sure it's your purpose. You will know if it is, it will be so clear and so obvious to you that you will not be able to stop the transition from helped to helper even if you wanted to. All the signs will be there. People you don't know will be forever walking across your path of life in need of your help. You will always feel that you must put other people before yourself. It's not a common occurrence, so don't think that you are going to have to give up your job to walk the earth and heal people. It doesn't work like that. There are only a few people that have such a duty on the earth plane, but you need to know about it just in case it's you!

4b Embracing their wisdom (helping others)

IF YOU DO FIND YOURSELF LUCKY ENOUGH to be someone who has discovered the ability for such a task hold on to your hat. It's life changing; it really is. One minute you're reading a spiritual book the next you are channelling through meditation, learning how to relax and finding yourself thrown into a world of spiritualism because you have a gift that you never knew you had. For some of you it may be very hard to deal with at first because your life is partly taken over by your need to pass on the wisdom from your guides. You will always know if you are going to be one of the few whose sole purpose on this earth is to help because it will be made so obvious to you. But be warned: If helping others is your purpose, you must keep it close to your heart. You will not have to shout out about it. The people you are destined to help will somehow just find their way to you. You won't have to do anything. It just happens that way. Always remember that. Don't talk about it down at your local pub, or in your dance class, or at a party. Let it just happen. Put it this way, if your new-found higher self had the ability to find you, then it will surely have the ability to create circumstances. Understand that when you are dealing with your guides, to help others, the knowledge and ability that comes from them is infinite, a never-ending place of pure belief, faith, love and wisdom.

It's so refreshing that many of you who yearn for a greater spiritual path. Doors will open for all of you who are destined for greater things. If only one of you reading this book becomes a helper of spiritual practice, then that would just be fantastic. If that's you, then well done, and good luck and God bless.

5a Discovering your purpose – relating to others

YOU WILL COME TO FIND that if it's your destiny to be a helper on the earth you will start to find it difficult to relate to people, even people that have been close to you for a long period of time. In this section we will talk about how you can overcome the hardship of being a healer within any spiritual practice.

As you are already aware, any significant change in anyone's personality will have advantages and disadvantages. The advantage of becoming a helper on this earth is that you also become free of the day-to-day relative pressures that life holds over you. The disadvantage of acquiring the gift of wisdom and knowledge is that you can be made to feel the odd one out, not necessarily by anyone else – unless you go telling the world about your new-found ability – but by yourself.

Imagine two Mini cars that were bought in the same year. They are identical. One day you decide to put a Porsche engine in one of the Minis. All of a sudden you have two cars that look the same, but on the inside they are very different. If you were driving the Mini with the new engine, firstly it would be very difficult not to go fast, as your new engine would probably seize up. Secondly, why would you want to go slow if you have a Porsche engine under the bonnet? This is what happens when you are given the gift of insight. You get the Porsche engine to deal with life's issues. You see people's problems incredibly clearly without even thinking about it. You step away, without even trying, from the old world to this new world, full of love, peace and understanding. But we are only human living in a world where the days can seem long and loneliness a burden. The harder you work for others, the greater your awareness becomes. You will find that as you walk your journey for others, times can be hard. Your ability will help you to overcome the pressures. This is something you, and only you, will have to deal with when the time comes.

Another key issue that you must be very aware of is that of the non-believer. The person or people trapped in their own world, often by choice, just waiting for the opportunity to bring you down, make you feel small and mock you. We must stand back and forgive but, once again, we are only human. While we remain in the shell we have been given we can always be hurt by the people who pursue those with the spiritual gift, only to try to crucify them.

Always think before you give any kind of help or advice. If you have had message after message after message for other people there is a pressure to inform the person in front of you. This is where helpers need to practise the art of silence.

People sometimes ask, "If the spirit world has an infinite bank of knowledge, then why would a guide put us in an unsafe situation where it could cause us problems in the future?" Well my answer to that is that there may be an infinite amount of knowledge that creates all and becomes everything but it is all about timing. We choose our moments. If it seems impossible to deliver the message, then save it for a later date. Do not leave yourself wide open; your guides may be testing you. They may want to see your strength of will or it may be that you did not close your chakras properly and an unwanted spirit crept into your conscious. Do not be fooled. When you discover anything in life, especially your purpose, there are not only people who find that threatening, but there are also many different unexplained events that occur in spiritually dedicated people's lives that are not always positive. Life is about good and bad; expect the two often to come side by side.

5b The seven-day hell

ET'S TALK ABOUT an issue that crops up usually for the helpers who go
onto the next stage of full-blown spiritualist, medium or clairvoyant.
What you're about to read is something that doesn't bear thinking about,
but has to be experienced if and when someone is taken to the next level.
I have spoken to many different mediums and spiritualists who have
experienced what I call the seven-day hell. It is a period of seven days and
nights where you are bombarded by pure negativity. The mediums in
question were only told afterwards, in what seemed like a visionary
message, that it was the ultimate test of good to see if they were able to
stand up to negativity. It's the old story of good versus evil. If you cannot
withstand the painfully mental time, or seven-day hell, you cannot go
further in your spiritual development as it is seen as not being your
destiny. But, if you can withstand the seven days of hell, which consists of
horrible visions and very negative thoughts, you will transcend onto your
next plane, the plane of full-blown helper. No pain, no gain. We can't all
be mediums and spiritualists, can we? Who would be the lawyers, the
doctors, the politicians and the mathematics teachers? Not that anyone of
those people couldn't have an ability to become a reader, but being a full-
time reader often means just that: full-time.

So, if your purpose in life is to play a part in helping others on this
earth you will come up against a lot of negativity on the way. This has
always been the case, the fight between good and evil. If you can fight,
fight until the bitter end. The world needs more and more spiritually
able people in it so we can dominate with the use of love and positivity
not with hatred, fear and negativity. If you are fortunate to get to the
point in your journey where you experience the seven-day hell, then you

are well on your way to a very fulfilling life. Do not let evil win. Be brave. Have no fear and keep your faith. You will be the victor.

6a Walking through to the other side

IF YOU HAVE MADE IT out of the seven-day hell and have managed to overcome all of the fear and negativity, then you will feel as though you are floating on air. You have made it! You have made it through to the other side where you literally feel as though you have God on your side. All of what you have learnt suddenly becomes so obvious that you're convinced you already knew all of it. Or you may question why what now seems like second nature to fully understand your new-found knowledge and wisdom, you didn't see it before. You see the clearing through the trees. When you think about it you can't know all that you would know as a full-blown reader. It would just be too much to take on board. But now that you have made it you can relax into the knowledge that you have gained; a true sense of what life is. You now hold so many unanswered questions of life. You must be very careful who you allow to see the gift of wisdom that you now hold within you.

You must also allow yourself time to just settle into the new you. Your journey into helping others will most probably be starting sooner than you think, so make the most of your own time. Just relax and try to get your head around the new you. Some people are born with the special gift of reading. However, a lot of you just have to go through a basic process to see if you're able to be a reader. Give yourself time to come to terms with your new gift. It's very important to do this. The first two to three weeks are critical in that this is when you could become afraid and freak yourself out. Stay calm. Be happy that you have new-found wisdom, and prepare for an incredible journey.

6b The journey

THE JOURNEY IS NOW ABOUT TO BEGIN and you need to be prepared as a reader. You'll need certain things. Start with a tape recorder, to tape any messages you give and a good stock of candles – red is for strength, purple for spirituality and pink for eternal love. Light the candles when you're doing a reading.

For some people the journey can start off bumpily, for others very smoothly. It all depends on how they deal with the presence of power and wisdom. You need to keep an eye on your awareness, making sure you stay focused and in control of any incoming messages.

The reader normally has people that will come to him or her through recommendation. Do not worry if you have just found you have the gift; your guides will send people to you. It might not be how you think. It hardly ever is. The most valuable thing about this journey is the surprise.

You will forever be surprised in what you find within the messages, what they mean and their purpose.

Some readers at this stage still like to go into a small meditation to get their messages for their clients. But as you progress, you fine-tune your reading ability until you no longer need to meditate. You will find that the more readings you do, the longer they will become. At first you may just have a few messages to give to someone. This may take about half an hour, until you find yourself that little bit further down your spiritual road and most likely reading for someone for one hour.

The more readings you do, the faster you will be able to understand what the messages mean to give to the person sitting in front of you. To translate the message, read on.

6c The real talent

TRANSLATING A MESSAGE from your spiritual guide is where the talent needs to be perfected.

Messages can come in many different forms. They can either be visual images from your crown chakra area, feelings that need to be put into words, or spoken words that come in the sound of your own voice – if you ever hear someone else's voice, go to a doctor. They are often given to you in visual snippets or in symbols, so it's important to be able to decipher between an actual image and a symbolic image. Nothing is ever as it seems.

As you work through a reading you will start to build a picture of what needs to be addressed in the person's life you are reading. Make sure you don't get confused between your own thoughts and the messages sent from your guides. Remember, it's always in your own voice. That talent takes time, but don't worry. You will master it. You will also find that your guides seem to plan your journey for you, nearly always starting with friends who are interested in spiritual matters or for test readings, before you're set free to read for strangers. Don't be afraid that you are going to be thrown in at the deep end. That very rarely happens with something as sensitive as spiritual advice.

Make sure you have opened and closed your chakra points correctly. Keep any possible negative energy from creeping into your reading by opening and closing your client's chakra points on their behalf, but do make them aware of this as they might prefer to open and close themselves.

7 Controlling your new-found wisdom

IF YOU ARE FORTUNATE to have found the path to the ultimate spiritual sanctuary then there are several factors that have to be honoured.

You have found yourself being a bearer of positive spiritual advice, to be aware, ready and available at any given time for the hearts and souls of others.

At times you will be sad and at times you will be happy, just like before your new-found awareness. You can still land yourself in hot water on many occasions if you're not careful even after you've developed your abilities. That's why self-control is a must when working within the world of spiritualism.

The beginning of your new journey is where you are most vulnerable to outer negative interferences. You must ensure that you use the prayer of protection as often as you can. You must do this to stop the negativity of the ego taking control of your mind. If you haven't protected yourself properly you may find yourself head to head with many people in social situations, fighting over words of who believes what. You have tapped into a much more advanced power of knowledge so you would naturally be the victor in all situations, but this is the kind of thinking you must avoid. Control the need to want to show people what you can do. Always remember to forgive. Not everyone has chosen to dedicate a major part of their life to increasing their abilities like you have. At first it is tough, but learn to say nothing. Let them always believe they are right and just walk away. You will never get through to anyone by shouting or arguing, especially regarding spiritual matters. What you must also remember is that maybe one in a thousand may think seriously about the possibilities of being somebody who is psychic. It really is just a small number of people planning their escape route out of the relative world in which they live. You will also come across other types of people who always read spiritual books, but never put anything into practice in their own life. They read the books, go to the seminars and maybe the odd psychic meeting and, hey presto!, they are psychic. It's important to remember that if you can't see that love is the key to all of this, then how can you achieve anything? I have met so many of these types of people and it is very hard to watch them fooling themselves into believing that they are someone they are not. I am not here to judge. I am merely here to give advice and if that means making you aware to watch out for the delusional people, then so be it.

It's also very important to make sure that you do not lose yourself in the spiritual world. People have been known to end up quite ill because they couldn't balance the two worlds. You must make sure you don't overwork yourself spiritually, by working to many hours in a row. Never do more than three hours of readings in a day. Once you have finished a reading no matter how small, finish it. Do not let your client or friend continue to ask more questions once you have closed your chakras and ended the reading. They will try. You must also give only what is given to you. Do not go back on your word. Whatever you say to your client is final. Sometimes your interpretation may change slightly, but the meaning and final outcome of any part of any reading should remain the same.

At times you may doubt. Some clients you have may not relate to anything you are telling them. But do not lose sight and faith in yourself. What you give is what you got, and that's all you can give.

At times you may end up very frustrated when nothing seems to be going right in a reading, but do not worry about that. Life has an amazing way of working itself out and the future is often the more fascinating because things are never as they seem. Someone you're reading for may be saying, "No. No. No," to every message you give them. But two months, six months, a year later or even the next day they may come back to you and say, "Oh my God, I don't believe it! Everything you said has just happened. You are amazing!!!" So, don't worry at the time if your accuracy seems a little off target.

Another piece of advice in controlling your wisdom is: try not to let the person you're reading for tell you too much about themselves. If they start to talk about their life, ask them to kindly stop. If you allow them to continue talking to you about themselves, it will, firstly, confuse your conscious mind when conflicting information comes through, and secondly, they will tell their friends you probably picked up most of the information you gave them in the reading by what they let slip. So, as you can see, it's best to ask them to say nothing after you have greeted them so that there is only one outcome to the reading. You will then come highly recommended.

There is not one spiritualist, medium or psychic out there who in the beginning didn't make all the mistakes we have been discussing. Now you have a head start on all other psychics who had to learn the hard way. Always remember to forgive, forgive, forgive, and to be humble, humble, humble. You will not go wrong if you continue to be that way in your everyday life. Control your new-found wisdom; do not let it control you.

8 The eleventh hour

HERE WE ARE just about to come to the end of chapter seven, and you may still not feel that you have gained the wisdom that is possible. You may be feeling that you have not accomplished. You may have not yet experienced any of what we have talked about in this chapter. Do not worry. The eleventh hour is about that final chance to put things right. You have what it takes, as does everyone. If you feel something is not clicking into place, then step back to the area in the book about which you feel cloudy. The eleventh hour is just as it states. Just as you think it's all over for you, it happens. The trust makes itself known to you.

But this eleventh hour has a slight twist. The twist is: if you haven't been honest with yourself, there will be no Step Eight.

We live in a society where we struggle for success. We cause ourselves undue heartache and pain over such trivial matters. Spiritualism is the answer: not to be the full-blown reader but to merely be in touch with yourself. The eleventh hour is your last chance to change the way you think about your purpose in life and the needs in your life. It's highly likely that, after everything written, you now want to be psychic. You have to be psychic. "This is great! Imagine the power I could have or what I could do with that kind of insight." But the reality is that you cannot be selfish with awareness. If you are thinking only of yourself, then you need to go back to the beginning of the book. Start again and read until you believe in you. It will be then, and only then, that you are ready, and it will be then, and only then, that your spiritual guide will take you seriously and allow you such a gift. Would you give such a gift to a blind man if his guide dog wouldn't even walk with him? We can be blind and will be guided, but only if we will guide the blind. It is about being thankful for small mercies. Being thankful for the air we breathe, the food on our table and the thoughts of love and sensitivity we give to others when putting them first.

You have the chance to make it at the eleventh hour, your eleventh hour. Make it for yourself and for others. Be free to be the owner of your spiritual sanctuary. Govern your needs and exercise positivity for a better world. Be the owner of your spiritual destiny. Walk the earth with peace and love in your heart, for without this, what do we really have?

Your Step

WE ARE FINALLY HERE. The step that everyone's been waiting for, the step with all the answers. Well, here is a surprise for you. This step is totally different to all the other steps. You have been told everything you need to know to become a better person on this planet. Now it's up to you. Step Eight. This step is totally yours. It's where you decide whether or not you have it, the desire to conquer your spiritual journey. The whole point of this book is not for you to have the answers of life handed to you on a plate, but to give you simple pieces of information that you will already know. This is about you, my friend. This is about your own self-discovery and belief. There can be no lazy, hand-it-to-me-on-a-plate type people being granted gifts of extreme vision. It just won't happen.

We can't learn from anything or anyone about our true higher self. You can be told everything you need to know, but without you first creating a pathway to your destiny and being it, you will stay where you are.

There will be many of you reading this last section in the hope of gaining some kind of magical interpretation of life. Sorry, no can do. You have to go right back to the beginning of the book to the introduction and author's note to understand why this is being written. If you want to better yourself and have just picked up the book and turned to this page, then go back. If you feel there is nothing for you to learn, no stone that needs to be turned over, no questions that need to be answered, then you should probably put the book down. This book is for people who want to learn how to be themselves, and to be happy, content, peaceful, understood and aware.

This step is all about you, about the fact that no matter what is said or done, the outcome of your spiritual success, your evolutionary transition is solely and totally, at the end of the day, down to you.

This book just gives you a glimpse of hope. By taking simple steps you can become a happier person, with a brighter outlook. The information herein may not be for everyone. It most probably isn't. But if it can show you just one thing, it is that you will find a new peace within.

Your journey of self-discovery starts here. Please use the following eight pages provided to complete your answer to your life. Make notes to keep, and to refer back to. By now, you will have understood that nobody can give you the answers to life – to your life – except you. That is why you, and only you, can complete your eighth step.

Look into yourself. It's there that you will see the truth of your purpose! Good luck on your journey.

Step 8: Your step

Step 8: Your step

Author's final note

There is a greater, more powerful being at work here,
within us, within our steps to heaven. Let the humble soul
we have been given, give respect to its wish.
God bless xxx

About the Author

Glyn Parry is a young, creative individual who has developed his own spiritual awareness to help him face the challenges that every day life brings as well as to aid him in his demanding career in music. He lives with his wife in London, England. This is his first book.

From Glyn Parry to his readers:
If at any time you would like to let me know how the book has helped you, please write to me at:

Glyn Parry
c/o Contact Publishing Ltd.
Suite 346
176 Finchley Road
London
NW3 6BT
UK

Contact Publishing

-.-. --- -. - .- -.-. -

Publishers of Innovative Ideas

Visit us at

www.contact-publishing.co.uk

for information about:

Readers

Latest book releases

Catalogue

Ordering our books online

Writers

www.contact-publishing.co.uk